ROOTED

CENTRAL ARKANSAS FARM & TABLE

LACEY THACKER & SARA MITCHELL

Support your farmers.
Sara Mitchell

Nothing like good, clean dirt—
_Lacey Thacker

Dedicated to:

*The growers, artisans, restaurateurs, and consumers
who participate in the local food economy.*

Table of Contents

INTRODUCTION

Growing your own food seems romantic. The idea of putting a seed in the soil, adding water and sunshine, and eventually reaping the fruit of the earth is downright primal.

Farmers are connected to their labor in ways many of us never get to experience. Food, after all, is the thing that keeps us alive.

That's what *Rooted* is all about—the stories of people who grow, produce, and sell food. We set out to record their dreams and their challenges. From the time we began interviewing, we encountered families who were in this together, working side by side—and we also encountered farms and businesses that had to completely pivot or close altogether due to the changing demands of the marketplace and the difficulty of a climate that doesn't allow for growing twelve months a year.

We met farmers who, despite well-known names, weren't making enough to be considered sustainable—for sustainable doesn't just mean growing practices that are good for the earth, but also means practices resulting in an income that will sustain a family. A number of farmers are working to improve their work-life balance by diversifying what they grow and where they sell.

For many years, Central Arkansas had only a handful of restaurants thinking about local food. But then, in the mid aughts, something changed. Today, it takes more than two hands to count the number of restaurants touting their efforts to buy local food, and it takes twice that many fingers to count the number of growers and influencers working to draw attention to the importance of local food to the local economy.

Arkansans take great pride in their roots. Not everyone in *Rooted* is an Arkansas native, but those highlighted are working toward the goal of making delicious food accessible, giving farmers a fair rate for their produce, and improving the lives of their employees and customers. There is a lot happening in the Natural State—in the soil and in the community. Agriculture has always been at the forefront of the state's economy, and today is no different. The new guard of growers in Arkansas has a modern vision of farming. It's much more biodiverse, more organic, and more connected to the community than ever before.

Jack Sundell of The Root Café calls it "deep local"—that group of people, so influential, who seem to all know each other. The more involved with local food we become, the more we *all* know each other.

The people, farms, and food artisans within these pages hardly create an exhaustive list. A number of others could have rightly been included. But, we limited ourselves to a relatively small circle in Central Arkansas, with a little grace distance given to meat farmers. As soon as you start expanding the circle, you find you're only a few miles from yet another quality producer.

In *Rooted*, we pay homage to some of those who helped create the Central Arkansas food scene we have today, and we invite you to, for a moment, imagine Central Arkansas without those people, restaurants, and farmers. Then, breathe a sigh of gratitude that they *are* here, doing work that daily improves our meals, our community, and our land.

Farmers, Farmer's, Farmers' . . . What kind of market is it?

Market goers have seen every iteration of the term "Farmers Market." Because there are so many opinions on the subject of where and if an apostrophe belongs, we've decided they're all correct—and none of them are correct.

According to the Associated Press, whose style guide rules most news organizations' decisions about apostrophes and other punctuation, *"farmers market"* is preferred, the idea being that it's a market made up of farmers.

But there are outliers—some prefer "farmer's market," as in, a market that belongs to the individual farmers who sell there. The Bernice Garden Farmers' Market swaps the apostrophe to create a market belonging to the collective of vendors who line up each Sunday from 10 am – 2 pm.

Whatever your thoughts on the subject, the important thing is that you attend a market and help support local farmers and vendors.

The Bernice Garden Farmers' Market
1401 Main Street, Little Rock
Sundays, 10am – 2pm, rain or shine
From April to November
Closed Labor Day weekend

The Hillcrest Farmers Market
2200 Kavanaugh Boulevard, Little Rock
Every Saturday
October to April, 8am – 12pm
May to September, 7am – 12pm

The Little Rock Farmers' Market
400 President Clinton Ave, Little Rock
Saturdays, 7pm – 3pm, rain or shine
From early May through late September

Westover Hills' Farmers Market
6400 Kavanaugh Boulevard, Little Rock
Tuesdays from 3:30pm – 6pm
May through September

The Market on Merrill
1525 Merrill Drive, Little Rock
Thursday mornings
From May through September

St. Joseph Farm Stand
6800 Camp Robinson Rd, North Little Rock
Saturday from 8am – 12pm
May through October

Barnhill Orchards Farm Stand
277 Sandhill Road, Lonoke
Daily from 8am – 6pm
From May through October

OTHER MARKETS

For locally-grown and produced goods, visit one of these specialty stores:

The Bramble Market
9325 Ferndale Cut Off Rd, Little Rock
Open Wednesday through Sunday

Me And McGee Market
10409 US-70, North Little Rock
Open Wednesday through Sunday

Old Crow General Store
17202 AR-5, Benton
Open Tuesday through Saturday

FEATURED PRODUCERS

ST. JOSEPH CENTER OF ARKANSAS
North Little Rock
Produce / Farm Store

HONEYSUCKLE MERCANTILE & CATTLE CO.
Rose Bud
Farm Store / Cattle

CAPI PECK
Little Rock
Restauranteur using local produce

BARNHILL ORCHARDS
Lonoke
Produce

THE ROOT CAFÉ
Little Rock
Restaurant using local produce

RATTLE'S GARDEN
Vilonia
Produce and Cut Flowers

SCOTT MCGEHEE
Little Rock
Restauranteur using local produce

LOBLOLLY CREAMERY
Little Rock
Ice Cream

ANITA DAVIS
Little Rock
Private Garden for Public Use

HEIFER INTERNATIONAL
Little Rock
Livestock / Education for Sustainable Living

JOSH HARDIN
Sheridan
Produce

MYLO COFFEE CO.
Little Rock
Coffee / Restaurant using local produce

RATCHFORD BUFFALO FARMS
Marshall
Buffalo Meat

WYE MOUNTAIN MUSHROOMS
Little Rock
Mushrooms

ROZARK HILLS COFFEE ROASTERIE
Rose Bud
Coffee

DUNBAR GARDEN
Little Rock
Produce

BEN POPE
Little Rock Children's Hospital
Produce

ACCESS GARDEN
Little Rock
Herbs

FARM GIRL MEATS
Perryville
Pork / Poultry / Beef

FEATURED LOCATIONS

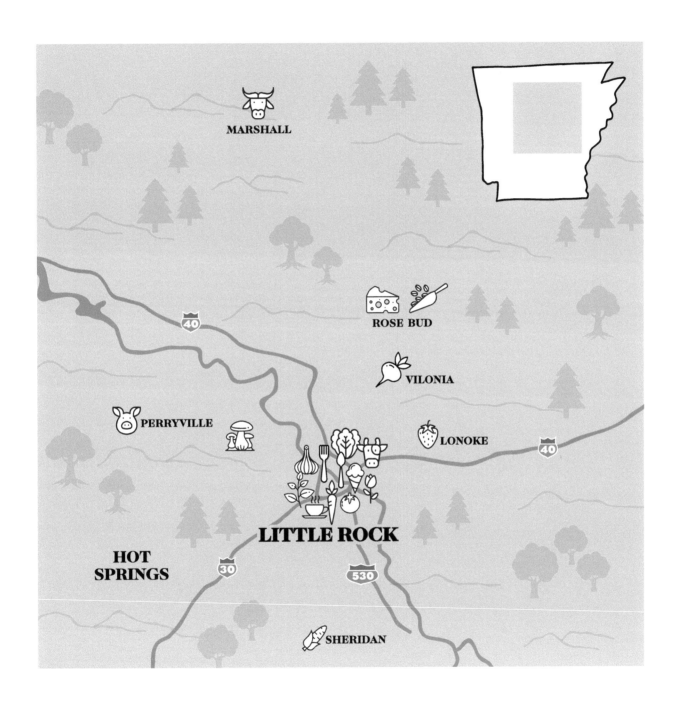

MARSHALL

ROSE BUD

VILONIA

PERRYVILLE

LONOKE

LITTLE ROCK

HOT SPRINGS

SHERIDAN

ST·JOSEPH'S·ORPHANAGE·
RT·REV·JNO·B·MORRIS·
LITTLE·ROCK·ARK·
CHAS·L·THOMPSON·ARCHITECT·

ST. JOSEPH CENTER OF ARKANSAS

Saint Fiacre, the patron saint of gardeners, offers his basket of produce and plenty for all who enter the St. Joseph Center of Arkansas garden. The statue, sculpted as a gift to St. Joseph by a family member of a former resident, is a constant reminder of the history and mission of St. Joseph's: to provide for those in need.

Originally an orphanage run by the Benedictine Sisters of St. Scholastica, St. Joseph and its century-old campus was founded by Bishop Morris. Morris envisioned a self-sustaining orphanage where residents were educated in the building's school and through working a farm. Today, the farm—comprised of sixty-three acres backing up to Camp Robinson in the Tanglewood neighborhood of North Little Rock—is sticking to its roots and establishing itself as an Arkansas gardening and farming destination.

This path hasn't been easy; farming rarely is. When the orphanage closed in the 70s, St. Joseph struggled with its identity—becoming a school, a day care center, a nursing home, and finally a retreat center. Building maintenance became more expensive, and the land suffered.

"When this place closed as an orphanage in the late 70s, that lost all the young labor," says Bert Turner, Central Arkansas Master Naturalist. "The pasture got overgrown. We are just trying to clear it out and get some light and grass on the ground."

The St. Joseph Center of Arkansas, SJCA, is a nonprofit group that formed in 2008 with the mission to save the property when the Catholic Diocese of Little Rock put it up for sale. Agreeing to a fifty-year lease with the Diocese, the SJCA understood the uniqueness and potential for the property, and embarked on a path to independence.

"We signed the lease in 2010 and tried to figure out who and what we wanted to be. We decided to focus our efforts on the outdoor assets," says Sandy DeCoursey, Executive Director of SJCA. "This is a community effort. This is for everybody."

SJCA started a community garden with their first grant of $5,000 from Fit2Live, an initiative developed by the city of North Little Rock and the North Little Rock School District aimed at curbing obesity in the city. At the time, no community gardens existed in North Little Rock. SJCA's ten beds quickly filled, an additional ten filled the next year, and again the following year.

SJCA saw a need not only for offering a *place* to grow food but an even greater need for resources and education on *how* to grow and what to do with that food once harvested. The former orphanage building uniquely positioned the property to house students and host more intensive trainings and workshops. The building has also been popular with artists who use it for studio space.

 Currently, SJCA hosts high tunnel workshops led by farmers Bobby Burrows and Travis DeLongchamp.

"They are basically just cheap greenhouses," Travis says. "They help farmers get to market earlier, so they are popular."

Realizing that most of the workshop attendees were looking to farm mainly for personal consumption, Bobby and Travis created a smaller, mobile version of the high tunnel which has been very popular.

"We are working with small farmers or backyard farmers, so the scale is too much," says SJCA's DeCoursey, "but the principles are the same." (See next page for Bobby and Travis inside high tunnel.)

Perched on a rocky hilltop with views of downtown Little Rock, SJCA now offers community beds to the public, a demonstration garden, and a hunger relief garden where produce is grown for those in need. Additional crops are sold to local restaurants and are available at the property's farm stand, open seasonally on Saturdays. Behind the farm stand is the greenhouse which also allows SJCA to grow earlier in the season. Added on to the former girls playhouse during the property's orphanage days, the greenhouse is an example of repurposing existing space while maintaining history at SJCA. Rockwork surrounding the pollinator garden was done by a former resident orphan who hoped to give back to his former home.

"We've just kinda utilized what was here," notes Sandy.

This collection of history that is scattered throughout the property definitely lends it a hallowed, spiritual feel. One recent resident, Heifer International's CEO Pierre Ferrari, was so drawn to the sacred environment that he rented a St. Joseph's room, simple and sparse as it would have been during the orphanage days, for four years to live in solidarity with Heifer's mission of eradicating poverty.

Sandy herself was pulled to SJCA by an outside force. She has been there a decade, a stint she took on with the idea that it would be one or two years.

"The holy spirit blew by and I forgot to duck," Sandy laughs. "It just got ahold of me."

Sandy also laughs when describing St. Joseph today. "We are the consummate orphanage. Half of our chickens have been dropped off on the side of the road. Our original intent was to grow heritage breed chickens and we soon realized that was unrealistic."

Several sheep and goats have also found their way to SJCA, needing a home. A lone Great Pyrenees, Peaches, serves as

the "guard dog" and sheepherder. Although SJCA hopes to eventually offer grass-fed beef, even the cattle are currently pets.

SJCA's future ambitions mirror its roots. With the loss of Arkansas GardenCorps, an AmeriCorps program which abated in Arkansas in 2018, there is a pressing need for education through school and community gardens. SJCA hopes to take up this mantle and is in the process of planning for a similar program through SJCA, funded by AmeriCorps. With funding, the possibilities are endless. SJCA aspires to become an educational center for farming with the capacity to host students and to train future farmers.

"I don't know where the future is leading," says Sandy. "But our vision for 2022 is to be a premier center for agritourism and education. We are on that path and we will see how far it gets us."

———

Location: North Little Rock
Known for: Education and agritourism
Site: stjosephcenter.org
Social: ❶@saintjosephcenter ❷◎@stjosephcenter

Like many farm families working multiple jobs to make a living, Raymond Daley works nights patrolling for the Rose Bud police department. There is little time for sleep. During his nocturnal patrol in the summer of 2018, he stumbled upon his family's next adventure. The "For Rent" sign in the former downtown post office building had just gone up. It was the middle of the night, and Ray could hardly wait for the family to wake so he could share his idea.

No strangers to risk-taking and outside-the-box thinking, the Daleys could be called serial farmtrepreneurs. A new project was just what the family needed. Originally dairy farmers with Honeysuckle Cattle Company, the Daleys also launched the state's first raw-milk cheese company, Honeysuckle Lane Cheese, in 2004. For years, the family had been exploring the idea of a farm store featuring their own products as well as those of other local growers.

Honeysuckle Mercantile opened in 2018 in the old post office. Featuring baked and local goods, the store has become the go-to stop for locals and travelers passing through Rose Bud. Homemade pastries, danishes, muffins, cookies, and cakes are the stars of this new venture—that is if you don't count the friendly family serving you. The market had always been a dream of the Daleys, a way to have a transparent, face-to-face relationship between customers and the farm. Now, Ray is not the only one getting little sleep. His wife, Cendie, and daughters Heather Cox and Amanda Galloway are getting up early to bake.

"That's a big change," laughs Heather. "We didn't even get up that early when we dairyed."

The store is as comforting as your grandmother's kitchen, complete with checkered tablecloths, wooden baskets, and cake stands brimming with fresh baked goods. The Daleys are putting the contacts they made in farming to good use as well. Along with their own beef, the store carries Ratchford Farms jerky (see page 52), Tammy Sue's Critters goats' milk products, and fruits and produce from local orchards and farms.

"We still feel like farmers," says Heather. "Our family background has led us to where we are. We have always stressed shopping locally and knowing where your food comes from.

Now, we can look to the people around us and see what they can produce and what we can carry."

The farm, where the Daleys have lived since 1993, is a picturesque setting of approximately one hundred acres just outside of Rose Bud that runs along a ridge with Beckett Mountain looming in the distance and the beef herd grazing behind a rustic barn. The long dirt drive is lined with fragrant honeysuckle in the spring and summer—the inspiration for the Honeysuckle moniker.

Having dairyed for twenty-eight years, it was bittersweet when Cendie sold her remaining dairy cows a month before opening the store. Saying goodbye to raw milk, and with it their raw milk cheese business, was the end of an era, but the Daleys had watched for years as dairying became more tightly regulated and small family dairies around Arkansas shuttered.

Cendie is the fourth generation of her family in Rose Bud, and Ray teases her that her roots run deeper than most. Ray's family is also from Arkansas but moved to several ranches throughout the state before his father became ranch manager at Heifer Project. He can be found today at Hillcrest Farmers Market selling farm fresh eggs and his own homegrown produce.

The Daleys were always looking for ways to have more stability on the farm. Since milk prices are set by the government, they are constantly fluctuating. Ray opted to add a beef herd along with Honeysuckle Lane Cheese, which developed a cult-like following in Central Arkansas.

Ray and his dad first learned to make cheese on a farm in Missouri. This well-known farm was later destroyed by a listeria outbreak involving green onions, which taught the Daleys a valuable lesson: the more you put in the cheese, the more can go wrong. That is the reason the Daleys stuck to four main varieties, grew their own jalapeños, and never used artificial coloring, opting for the annatto seed for orange color. Ray laughs and admits that he was often asked, especially with the Colby cheese, "How do you make that cheese white?" He responded, "The cheese is naturally white. We add natural color to our yellow cheddar."

The Daleys will admit they still miss the cheese. Honeysuckle Lane was churning out 400 gallons a week at its peak and was even being served in several restaurants. But the Daleys were tired. Cendie had long been in charge of the milking. She knew every cow's name and the best ways to calm them. Some mornings, Cendie's milk pipelines were frozen. The milking time already consumed much of her day. Frozen pipes meant extra time thawing them because the cows had to be milked, twice a day, no matter what. There were no family vacations. Her two daughters, Heather and Amanda, were grown and living their own lives, and she was always working. The final straw was when Cendie's mother was diagnosed with Stage 4 ovarian cancer and moved to the farm so Cendie could care for her.

"Raymond kept asking if I was tired, and I kept telling him, 'No, these are my babies,'" Cendie says, referring to her milk cows. Friends would offer to help with feeding the herd, but Cendie knew her "babies" wouldn't go to just anyone.

"You don't just put a milker on them. You have to look at their udders to make sure nothing is wrong. Feeding is the easy part," Cendie says.

A beef herd does not operate like a dairy herd. It is far less time consuming and requires less care. Every family member now has a hand in caring for the beef herd, but that usually just involves feeding. The beef herd is now the only cattle on the farm.

"Dairy cows have a different life than a beef cow, a longer life, but also, there is a personal connection. You are with them twice a day. It was a change for us when we started with the beef herd. We drive out and check them and feed them hay, but it's not that personal level like the dairy cows," says Heather.

Another reason the Daleys were tired: they had been campaigning for over a year to persuade Arkansas legislators to allow the sale of raw milk. Raw milk—milk that has not been pasteurized and exists in its natural state—is a controversial product due to the belief that bad bacteria can grow in milk and the heating process of pasteurization kills these bacteria. Proponents of raw milk believe the pasteurization process also destroys much of the good bacteria and nutritional value of milk. Equipment to pasteurize milk is also expensive and cost-prohibitive to small dairies like the Daleys'. The Daleys had always consumed their own Grade A dairy milk. They knew everything that went into their cows. They did not use any hormones and only treated with antibiotics if the cow was sick, disposing of the cow's milk until the antibiotic cycle was complete. The Daleys had worked in conjunction with the Arkansas Health Department to develop guidelines and establish regulations for raw milk cheese because Honeysuckle Lane Cheese was the first raw milk cheese producer in the state.

In 2013, state legislators passed a law allowing the sale of raw milk, but it could only be sold on farms, and this was the ruling that remained in 2015. This was a blow to the Daleys, who had hoped to sell raw milk in stores and markets, expanding their offerings to cheese and raw milk. Around this time, the idea of a store started being discussed between family members.

"In farming, you have to stay so relevant," says Heather. "You have to change to what people want to stay in it."

Cendie's mother responded well to cancer treatments, and Cendie became a grandmother to Heather's son, Jasper. What better place to raise a grandson than on a farm? Nathan, Heather's husband, had been a milk hand on the farm for years before he and Heather married. Heather jokes that he married her for the farm, but in a serious tone admits, "This was his home, too." They both agreed that they wanted to raise Jasper around animals. It's one thing to tell your child that a cow says "moo," and another thing to have a pet cow that moos to him every day.

"Nate and I knew we wanted Jasper to be raised like we were. We wanted him to play in the mud, be around animals, and learn all that animals teach you."

Jasper begins the sixth generation of this family in Rose Bud, and Cendie's longtime dream of a family compound is closer to coming true. Heather's sister Amanda and her husband Travis have moved back to the farm, living in the original cheese plant, which has been converted into a bunkhouse. Travis jokes that they need to run over to "Mom-Mart," Cendie and Ray's house, for some supplies, but Cendie wouldn't have it any other way.

Heather and Amanda are also bringing new skills to the business. Heather jokes that she is just learning the social media world, but her millennial skills are already paying off. Honeysuckle Mercantile, on Instagram and Facebook, is reaching people from across the country through its online presence.

"Heather's our planner," says Cendie. "The whole Facebook thing, I would never do it." A trial giveaway on social media ended up reaching more people than the Daleys had planned, convincing Heather that online marketing is the way to go now. Heather admits that she as grand plans. Having seen her parents work hard for so long has taught her a strong work ethic.

> ## "It's one thing to tell your child that a cow says 'moo,' and another thing to have a pet cow that moos to him every day."

"It's a lot of work, but it's exciting," Heather claims. "We've found that if we can offer more, it makes people more apt to drive a little farther. The more we can produce on the farm, the better."

Neighbors and friends are also benefiting from the Mercantile, something the Daleys are proud to share. From the beginning, the goal has always been to create a community around farming and understanding where your food is grown.

"People are more concerned with where their food is coming from, how it's made, who's making it. Those are our customers," admits Heather. "Our customers are not the ones that go buy off the shelf at WalMart and don't care. It's a niche market."

____

Location: Rose Bud
Known for: Baked and local goods
Social: ⓕ@honeysucklemerc

CAPI PECK

Trio's Restaurant founder Capi Peck's life reads like a fairytale. Raised in the famed Sam Peck Hotel in downtown Little Rock (now known as the Hotel Frederica), Capi was as much a fixture of the hallowed halls as former Governor Winthrop Rockefeller, who lived at the hotel from 1953–1955 after leaving New York. A renowned destination from the late 30s to early 70s, Capi could be found among the civilized guests operating the switchboard, refining her palette on oysters shipped in for the hotel restaurant, the Terrace Room, and spying on the city's movers and shakers in the bar, After Five. Capi's grandparents, Sam and Henrietta Peck, lived in a penthouse on the sixth floor of the hotel, and when Capi was only fifteen she had her own apartment on the grounds. Hospitality, entertaining, and travel were all Capi knew, and she would only later learn how uniquely cultured her family was.

"That's where I fell in love with hospitality," says Capi. "It was a great way to grow up. In the 50s and 60s, Little Rock was not very cosmopolitan, but I got to meet a lot of interesting people that would travel through here. It was close to the federal building and the Arkansas State Capitol. There was a lot of wheeling and dealing. I was exposed to a lot of things that a young girl was just not exposed to in Arkansas in that era."

Capi admits that opening a restaurant was never on her radar. She did not attend culinary school, but she had developed a passion for cooking through her family and her travels. It seemed a natural fit to everyone else that the family's fourth generation in Arkansas hospitality would continue the tradition. Encouraged by a friend after the friend tasted Capi's food at a party, Capi opened a gourmet to-go deli and retail shop in 1986 in the original Trio's space at Pavilion in the Park, becoming one of the building's first tenants.

"When we were looking for a space, everyone would say, 'Oh, that's just way too far west,' and now this kind of seems like midtown," Capi laughs.

The catering side of the business quickly took off and Capi and then-husband Brent realized the location and parking were not ideal for a grab-and-go restaurant. They transitioned to a full-service restaurant with staff and focused on Capi's Mexican-inspired food. There were also some nods to her family. The popular Peck Salad with bacon, roasted chicken, and almonds, dressed with a signature vinaigrette, was a salad created by Sam Peck and served at the hotel. Sam Peck was adventurous with his food. He brought the first Caesar salad to Little Rock after he was served one tableside in California. Following Sam, Capi is known for bold flavors and daring cooking, a departure from the Southern staples found in most Little Rock restaurants at the time she opened Trio's.

Capi also built a reputation for delivering fresh, innovative cuisine using local produce, a tradition which started with a patron. A master gardener who was a regular in the restaurant mentioned that she grew herbs and lettuces and asked Capi if she would be interested in trying some. This was in the late 80s, and it would help launch Capi's staunch philosophy of using locally-grown ingredients to deliver the highest quality product. She was one of the first in Central Arkansas to be openly driven by these values.

"Some people make a very conscious decision as to where they spend their dining dollars," Capi says. "I want to know where things come from. We are what we eat. I want to know what I put in my body."

Capi started working with local grower Sue's Garden in the 90s and bought thousands of pounds of strawberries and carbon tomatoes. She also developed relationships with Armstead Farm, Barnhill Orchards, Rabbit Ridge, and local mushroom foragers. She has had a long relationship with Alan Leveritt's India Blue Farm, known for its heirloom tomatoes.

"Everybody knows a tomato shipped in looks like a tomato but doesn't taste like a tomato," says Capi. "I'm fortunate in that my clientele will pay a little more if I'm using organic and local. They understand that it's going to taste better but it's going to cost a little more."

Capi admits it would be much easier for her to order her produce from a large provider and have a standard menu, but it is not what her customers expect. She is grateful that farmers are now embracing technology, texting her lists of available produce, and willing to come to her at the restaurant. A master at time management, Capi appreciates this efficiency.

"It's so much easier now. I can remember ten or twelve years ago, it would take me all day Saturday just to go around to the different markets and make runs in my car buying produce for the week," Capi says.

She still enjoys visiting the markets and meeting farmers, since what is in style, even in food, is constantly changing. A popular feature on Trio's menu is the summer "Farmer's Market Splendor" where Capi will create a dish based on what she finds at the market. Featuring items provided by local farmers, the splendor may have an heirloom caprese, purple hull peas, okra fritters, or a squash medley. It all depends on what is in season and what Capi can create.

"We are what we eat. I want to know what I put in my body."

Capi and Brent were also big proponents of recycling and incorporating environmentally sustainable practices in the business when few were operating this way. Capi is responsible for helping to launch Little Rock's first recycling program, and she and Brent formed AGRA, the Arkansas Green Restaurant Alliance, in the 90s. An idea ahead of its time, the goal was for restaurants to form a co-op to buy expensive compostable packaging in bulk, ban Styrofoam and unnecessary plastic from member restaurants, and make environmentally responsible choices.

"I'd be more profitable if I wasn't doing those things. Honestly, it takes a lot more energy and it costs a lot more, but I bought into it a long time ago. It's the way I want to do business."

In the kitchen, Capi now focuses on menu planning and expediting at Trio's. It's been many years since she has cooked on the line, but she mentored Shanna Merriweather, Trio's executive chef of nearly two decades. As the expeditor, Capi checks the outgoing plates, confirms orders, and acts as

the conductor of the kitchen orchestra—a performance she would have seen nightly at the Terrace Room of the Sam Peck Hotel.

Capi is most humbled by and proud of her staff's longevity. She has several employees who have been with her for more than fifteen years. One of her first employees, who started at Trio's as a sophomore at J.A. Fair High School, is still with her.

"This has been his only job," Capi marvels. "I am so proud of that."

It's a testament to Capi and the way she chooses to run her business. She always takes the time to listen, teach, and learn. Relinquishing control of her restaurant to her trusted staff has freed up time for additional projects including an unexpected turn to local politics. Encouraged by her fellow restaurateur and Little Rock Vice-Mayor Kathy Webb, Capi, whose initial reaction to entering politics was "Hell no!" ran for, and won, a seat as City Director of Ward 4.

"It is the ultimate way to give back to Little Rock," Capi says. "I love this place so much. I grew up here. My business is here. I have been successful because of the community."

Not surprisingly, many of Capi's most passionate initiatives revolve around food and hospitality. Food, after all, is often a way to bring people together. She has been on the Little Rock Advertising and Promotion Commission for a decade, is active in the Arkansas Hunger Relief Alliance, and is an advocate for affordable housing for low-income families and those without homes.

Now that she has learned the ins and outs of the local government, which she describes as "huge," it's clear this form of leadership has become a new passion and the next chapter in her tale.

———

Location: Little Rock
Known for: Bold flavors and locally-sourced ingredients
Site: triosrestaurant.com
Social: ❶❷⊙ @trioslr

BARNHILL ORCHARDS

"I baby these things," laughs Barnhill Orchards' Rex Barnhill when describing his strawberries. "I put a blanket on them when it's cold; I feed them and make sure everybody is happy. A happy plant makes a happy berry."

Many Arkansans would argue that Barnhill has the happiest berries in the state. So popular are Rex's berries that the farm's phone rings constantly during strawberry season, and the white and red delivery truck gets stopped all over town with pleas for any berries that can be spared.

On the day we visit, the strawberry plants have about had it, and they'll be pulled later that afternoon. Rex and his sister Ekko invite us to try one, and they are luscious, juicier than any found in a store. Picking them directly from the field only enhances the experience, Ekko noting that the curling leaves on the top of the berry mean it is at its peak ripeness.

But Barnhill didn't start out raising berries. The farm originally began as a peach and pecan orchard. In 1980, Bob Barnhill, a retired military colonel, and his wife, Carlotta, purchased the 100 acres in an area of Cabot known as the sandhills. The Barnhill's large family of seven lived in the original farmhouse, which dates back to the early 1900s. The Barnhills later purchased an additional fifty acres for the peach orchard. Realizing their most precious resources were time and family, not one inch of the property went to waste. This is why you will still find pecan and peach trees peppered throughout the property. The Barnhills determined that wherever there was space, they would plant.

The Barnhills also soon realized that the sandhills beneath their feet had a unique advantage over other farms. The sandy soil and the rise in the hills provided better drainage and minerals for crops. Fruits such as strawberries, blackberries, and blueberries flourished along with summer and fall vegetables like tomatoes, new potatoes, lettuces, and squash. Ekko Barnhill, the youngest of Bob and Carlotta's children and their only daughter, believes this is what makes their strawberries special.

"The sandy soil makes the berries sweeter," claims Ekko. "Fruit is what sells on a farm. We bring that sign out and people around here know we have berries. Particularly when the kids come in, they put their hands on the fruit and say 'Mom, this looks good.' They aren't grabbing for the squash," says Ekko.

The sign Ekko is referencing is another essential example of efficiency and resourcefulness that is the hallmark of this farm. The backboard of the "sign" is an old cotton wagon, which the Barnhills can tow out during the season and park along Highway 89. The red hand-painted "STRAW" in "STRAWBERRIES" can be flipped and replaced with "BLACK" when blackberries are in season after the strawberries.

The farm has been and continues to be a family-run business. Along with his "babies" in the field, you can find all of Rex's real babies working the farm. His three daughters work the corner market, sort the produce, and make deliveries to restaurants and buyers. You can find them in Carhartts with bushels of onions in their lap before heading in to study for a test, all three pursuing medical degrees. Rex's son also works in the fields. Rex's daughters and son, along with their cousins, comprise the third generation and future of the farm.

"Every day is a holiday when you can be outside and be with your family," says Ekko. "That's a blessing, that we are going to be able to pass this on."

With help from their aunt Ekko, the girls are also implementing fresh ideas such as farm boxes—think a co-op box where you pick the contents—and using technology to expand customer options and improve delivery.

Ekko and the girls will text local restaurants on their way into Little Rock letting them know what they have picked in the last week, and several chefs will build their menus around what is fresh. "The vegetables don't stop growing," says Ekko. "Providing fresh, quality produce is what we do best."

Stephanos Mylonas, owner of Mylo Coffee in Hillcrest, appreciates the efficiency of texts and photographs (see page 43). With a picture, Mylonas can see the produce and determine whether or not he wants to purchase what Barnhill is offering, all while keeping an eye on his busy kitchen.

It's this mindset and flexibility that chefs appreciate about Barnhill. Izard Chocolates (see page 47) wanted to do a chocolate dipped strawberry for Valentine's Day, so Barnhill planted rows of day-neutral strawberries, which hold their shape and size better than a field strawberry and are more desirable for chocolate.

The Barnhills actually prefer knowing ahead of time what to plant. They'd rather plant a crop that's destined for a buyer than guess each season what people will want. One example of this is the public schools. The Barnhills work with Beebe, Cabot, North Little Rock, and Searcy schools to provide farm-to-school produce. This way schools are getting fresh lettuce, squash, and fruit instead of produce shipped in from out of state.

Ekko's business savvy has landed her some large restaurant accounts as well. In 2015, the owner of David's Burgers met her at a farmer's market and commented on some of her lettuce. Not missing a beat, Ekko insisted he should use green frill lettuce, known for its quality, in his burgers. She sent him home with some to munch on. He returned the next day and placed an order for green frill lettuce to be used in his restaurants.

Not only do the Barnhills pay attention to what their customers want, they listen to what the land needs. "Our land is our greatest resource, you can't just plant once and pick forever," Rex says. "You have to move to another field. We are stewards of the land. It's kind of like the Boy Scouts — you want to leave it better than when you got here."

It has taken a lot of trial and error, but Rex has figured out how to maintain the land and prepare the soil for each harvest. After a field has been picked, the Barnhills put in a cover crop to keep the soil from eroding. Rex prefers a tall

Sudan grass that chops up well when he mows it. He uses this organic matter to fertilize his next crop.

The Barnhills have also created an irrigation system from a pond on the property to water the fields, conserving water. This homemade system is run using a Honda motor with a pull-start that cranks like a lawn mower. Nutrients can also be fed into the system snaking its way through each row in the field. Rex can put plugs in different lines to keep water from going to certain crops. He even invented an ingenious way to run the system, keeping him from having to travel to the back of the property to shut off the water.

"The best thing I've ever done was figure out that I could just put a certain amount of gas in the engine, and it shuts off on its own," Rex says, smiling. "I never have to come back and turn it off!"

Rex has learned a thing or two about farming from his dad, Bob, whom he calls "Daddy Bob." He also jokes that seven years in college and a geology degree helped. His knowledge of chemistry is impressive, but Rex humbly suggests that there are plenty of books that can provide the same Rex credits his dad with the success of the farm, saying, "Daddy built this farm from nothing to what it is today."

Barnhill practices successive planting in order to grow as much of the year as possible. Hoop houses and a structure the Barnhills refer to as a "high tunnel," with plastic siding that can be raised or lowered, help them control the temperature over crops in the hot summer months and during the cooler fall allowing them to plant earlier, and later, in the season. The Barnhills even reuse the plastic used in this process.

"You cannot rely on mother nature," reminds Ekko. "If it is a crop, we would rather be the one to control what it gets. We give it all the water we want to give it, the vitamins we want to give it."

Not only do you need to pay attention to temperature, irrigation, and nutrients, farmers must also consider wind and rain and how they will impact the crop's growth and strength. Daddy Bob plants rows and rows of beautiful heir-

loom tomatoes in the high tunnel, which allows him to more effectively control all the variables.

"You want to have your product when nobody else has it," Ekko claims. "If we can sell out of season, whether early or late, it's a good thing."

The Barnhills are exemplary stewards of the land, as well as stewards of their community. They have hosted school field trips and are always willing to meet with chefs or buyers who want to see where their food is grown. After the pecan harvest, several locals bring their pecans to Barnhill's shelling machine to be shelled and sorted. They get busy right before Christmas because many families like to give the pecans as gifts.

 A commitment to giving back extends much further into the family history. Between Bob and his five children, the family has a total of more than 100 years of military service and each of the five children served our country. Rex has thirty-two years of service in the National Guard. Two of his children also serve in the National Guard, in the Medical Corp and Engineering. Barnhill Orchards is certified Homegrown By Heroes, a program that ensures the agricultural product is produced by a U.S. military veteran. The Barnhills are proud of their service and strongly support military veterans.

If you find yourself driving I-40, be sure to take the Remington exit and drive the approximate six miles to the corner market. The newly enclosed market sells all of the Barnhill's goods plus those of some other nearby vendors. You will find the freshest fruit and vegetables around, brought to you by a family who insists on farming the way nature intended. You will likely also meet a Barnhill. They work sunup to sundown, and usually after that too.

———

Location: Lonoke
Known for: Berries and fresh produce
Site: barnhillorchards.com
Social: ❶@BarnhillOrchards

Breakfast at The Root Café is a culinary and cultural experience, be it Sunday brunch or the regular weekday menu. There's often a line of hungry customers out the door, waiting to place their orders and snag a table. Waiting diners sometimes sneak to the front and grab a steaming mug of coffee for their wait in the morning air. For frequent guests, it's more common than not to run into someone familiar.

Owned by husband and wife team Jack Sundell and Corri Bristow-Sundell, The Root Café is more than a place to eat; it's a place for people to enjoy community. The space was intended for people who live in Little Rock to connect with others. Jack Sundell explains, "We see groups that meet on a particular day of the week. Some people have been coming here for eight years, the entire time we've been open. We've watched their kids grow from being ten years old to eighteen years old." That concept is why The Root's mission statement is: "Building Community Through Food."

The Root's mission statement is, "Building Community Through Food."

It's a source of pride, the Sundells share, when someone from out of town comes to their restaurant and has a good experience. While working on opening the Café they visited cities across the US and found that the atmosphere of their experience in the city would be colored by the places they ate and the experiences they had around food. "If we were able to do that for somebody visiting Little Rock, then that's a really great thing," Jack says. And they are providing this for visitors—it's not uncommon to overhear someone in line mentioning that they'd heard about The Root and made a special pit stop on a trip to visit the eatery. When a new visitor wonders out loud what a banh mi sandwich is, a regular will often step in and explain—and then continue to talk about the entire menu as if it were their restaurant.

Before The Root was The Root, it was Sweden Creme, a dairy bar that ran from the 1960s to the 1990s. Anita Davis, sometimes called the "fairy godmother of South Main," the revitalizing neighborhood in which The Root is located,

owned the building when Jack and Corri were beginning to think about where they would house their restaurant (see page 35). As it turns out, Anita was looking for a focus on local food and hoped to help something of a startup, so when Jack and Corri reached out, it was a perfect fit. "She's been very good to us," Corri says.

The Root's thematic tie is traditional Southern staples, particularly in regard to breakfast and dinner. Lunch is a bit more varied, with items such as the Banh Mi Sandwich, a great burger, and a couple of bratwurst choices. Their mission is to consistently source as much local food as possible. Jack and Corri refer to the network of people involved in local food as "deep local." In some way, most participants are connected to each other. If one doesn't have another's cell phone number, they know someone who does.

"It's hard to run a restaurant without onions and carrots," Jack says, so while The Root only uses locally-grown tomatoes, for example, they're a bit more flexible on staple root vegetables, which they use in substantial enough quantities that they must occasionally rely on Whole Foods to fill the gaps.

BEFORE JACK AND CORRI WERE JACK AND CORRI

Before the Sundells began the restaurant, before they were even a couple, they were both food people.

Jack, the middle of three brothers, grew up in Monticello, where his father was a botanist at the University of Arkansas at Monticello. His mother, who sometimes worked at the library, cooked nearly every meal the family ate. They ate breakfast together as a family, and she would pack lunches for everyone, every day—unless, Jack says, they ". . . actually wanted to eat whatever it was . . . a square of pizza or taco salad at school." He credits their regular family time around the table as having a big impact on his desire to open a restaurant. It was his later experiences in the Peace Corps that led him to start thinking about local food. In Morocco, he saw how a family owning a flock of chickens or a cow directly impacted their ability to control their food supply. While visiting the local market—which most closely resembled a farmer's market back home—Jack discovered the real impact

of seasonality. Pomegranates, which were in season when he first arrived in Morocco, went out of season a month after he arrived, and he didn't see them again until a year later. "It was really one of the first times I experienced the importance of seasonal food and how wonderful it can be to just eat as much of something as you can while it's in season," he says.

After returning home, Jack's excitement about the idea of local food led him to the Heifer Ranch, where so many Arkansas farmers and foodies are incubated. His focus was on the livestock management program. His time at the ranch led to an interest in cooking, informed by group dinners and

potlucks the volunteers put together. The ranch also raised and processed chickens directly on the ranch, where they were then served in the cafeteria.

Corri spent summers as a child with her dad's parents in DeKalb, Texas, where they had a few cows along with a large kitchen garden and fruit trees. Corri and her cousins spent time helping out in the garden, sometimes digging potatoes and selling them by the side of the road. "We would all sit around and snap purple hull peas together," she remembers.

Corri often found herself revisiting those experiences in Texas while working to open the restaurant. "I remember [in the early days of the restaurant] having those big bags of peas on the dining room table and inviting friends over to sit around the table, tell stories, and snap peas," Corri says. Jack adds, "We were so, so naïve because we were thinking—" Corri jumps in— "those peas were going to last us a year." Finishing each other's sentences is common in conversation with Jack and Corri. One gets the idea that they have cultivated shared experiences into memories made complete only when they are together to contribute to the remembering.

It was Jack who originally developed the idea of opening a restaurant, but he met Corri at an art show early into the idea's development. They later sat down at Community Bakery to discuss the possibilities for the then-dream of The Root Café. One thing was certain: They would need money. Catering and food preservation workshops were the answer. The couple fundraised for several years to build capital for the restaurant's opening. While it initially felt like Jack's idea that she was helping with, Corri says she now feels equal ownership.

As with many new business ventures, during the first year or two Corri says the couple ate "so much take out." Before opening, they frequently invited visitors to potlucks at their home, but that halted during the restaurant's early years. Now, having been open since 2011, Jack notes that it's been fun rediscovering old passions and making time for exercise and friend-gatherings unrelated to work or kids—the couple now has twin sons. "I think the next frontier for me is learning to not feel guilty spending time away. Maybe I'm a workaholic," Jack says.

THE NEXT PHASE

In 2015, The Root received a grant for $150,000 from Chase's Mission Main Street Project which allowed them to execute an expansion of their dining space as well as the kitchen space. In the spring of 2017, The Root Café completed their addition and opened for dinner. The new dining space was built from, of all things, twenty-foot long shipping containers. During the expansion, Jack, Corri, and available help would come in on Mondays, make a huge mess, then clean from 6 p.m. until midnight before opening for breakfast the next morning. One Tuesday morning during construction, the couple didn't leave the restaurant until 1:30 a.m., and Corri says it really felt "like the old days."

Jack and Corri hope The Root serves as home for a series of experiences centered around food and community. Local food is just the conversation starter to local as a lifestyle in which people get to know their neighbors and become active in the community. Local food is the gateway to a local life—with regular events that help people meet each other, help make them excited about living in Little Rock and making it a place people want to come and visit—and leave feeling that they had a unique experience.

 In the fall of 2018, Jack and Corri joined forces with Cesar Bordon-Avalos, longtime kitchen manager of The Root Café, and his wife, Adelia Kittrell, to open Dos Rocas Beer & Tacos on South Main in Little Rock. Dos Rocas, which means "two rocks" in Spanish, is an homage to both Cesar's birthplace of Itá (which means "rock" in Guaraní, a native Paraguayan language) and Little Rock. Dos Rocas serves Latin American street food in a casual, family friendly environment, plus the best of Arkansas craft beer and Mexican and other Latin-American-inspired cocktails.

———

Location: Little Rock
Known for: Seasonal cooking from local ingredients, providing a gathering place for the community
Site: therootcafe.org
Social: ◉@therootcafe 🐦@therootcafelr ⨍@rootcafe

Tara Stainton was a pole vaulter in college; at the time, it was a relatively new sport for women. At a track meet a month before graduating in 2000, she met a group of pole vaulters who trained at a facility in Jonesboro. They and Tara hit it off, and it made her realize that, after only having spent two years in the sport, she just wasn't done.

After returning from the track meet, she called Arkansas State University to find out whether they would accept her for their masters program in education so she could train at the Jonesboro facility. At the end of the summer, she packed up and moved to Arkansas—where, she says, nothing is similar to Iowa.

After graduate school, Tara worked for the city of Jonesboro for a couple of years running their youth sports program. She had purchased her grandparents' farm in Iowa and was planning a move home in six months. "Then I met my husband, and life took another direction," she says.

"I spent the first three years of our marriage waiting tables in the mornings at a restaurant down the road, then farmed in the afternoons," Tara recalls. As a self-described self-taught farmer, Tara spent the first several years of her growing career learning how to grow vegetables. Most of her knowledge came from books and "the rabbit hole that is the internet."

Tara grew up in the middle of Iowa; her extended family was all row crop farmers. Tara's parents grew a garden until she was three years old, and they began gardening again after she went to college. "I said to my mother, 'You would have saved a lot of money on me going to school had you ever had a garden when I was old enough to participate in it.'" But they didn't, and so Tara never imagined she'd go into growing food. She planned to become a teacher, but instead, Rattle's Garden was unexpectedly born.

Today, Tara and her husband, Robert, whom she met through a mutual friend when Robert was calf-roping in the rodeo, live on forty-five acres near Vilonia. Fifteen of those acres are certified organic. At any given time, Tara has five acres planted, with the other ten in use as rotational space.

When Tara and Robert married nearly fourteen years ago, they'd just purchased land and begun building a home with no intention of growing food. Back then, her husband worked out of town for six or eight weeks at a stretch. It was just Tara and their five dogs much of the time. One day, she was walking through Barnes & Noble, and a book caught her eye—*Harvest for Hope: A Guide to Mindful Eating* by Jane Goodall. "That was the first time I ever heard the words sustainable or organic or anything like that." Tara spent the next few weeks reading about organic farms, and by the time her husband returned, she says, "I was converted."

Tara tells people it was almost like a religious awakening. "I fell for organic hard, and I believe in it. I've known since the beginning that if we were going to do this, this is the way I wanted to grow," she says.

Rattle's Garden began in 2006, and it was in the third year, 2008, that the garden began selling vegetables. It was also the year Conway Locally Grown, an online farmer's market, began. Through selling with Conway Locally Grown, Tara discovered a network of growers who helped steer her in a sustainable selling direction. At the time, she was one of the only farmers looking to grow organically, but she took the advice she was given from conventional farmers and considered how she could apply it toward organic growing.

A SPECIAL MARKET

Rattle's Garden grows diversified specialty vegetables, which basically amounts to, well, a lot of vegetables. The garden also grows cut flowers to sell at the Hillcrest Farmers Market. In addition to market sales, Rattle's Garden has over 100 families who participate in their farm share program for ten weeks in the summer and six weeks in the fall. The program began six years ago as a way to sustain their operation while decreasing the need for Tara to go to Little Rock. "One of the conditions I had for my husband was that I didn't want to drive into Little Rock for work. And the year before we started our farm share program, I was driving into Little Rock for The Bernice Garden Farmers' Market, Westover Hills' Farmers Market, the Sherwood Farmers Market, and the Hillcrest Farmers Market. So that was Sunday, Tuesday, Thursday, and Saturday I was commuting to farmers markets." The situation was untenable. The farm share program allowed Rattle's

Garden to reach out to the Vilonia community and develop a farm model that was sustainable for Tara and her family.

Customers can collect their farm boxes from three locations: directly at the farm (which about three-quarters of customers choose), the Hillcrest Farmers Market, or the Little Rock residence of Julie Majors. Tara says Julie has been instrumental in supporting local farmers, even growing her own small network of followers. Three years ago, Rattle's Garden began offering a pickup location at her house, and Julie handles everything after the food is dropped off.

The farm is Tara's full-time job. As the first certified organic farm in Faulkner County, Rattle's Garden does a lot of outreach in organic education. Over the last seven years, she's hosted twenty-six interns through a partnership with Hendrix College, and until recently, was the chair of the New South Co-op board of directors (see page 37)w. Her original interest in joining the co-op had a lot to do with that outreach and education. "I didn't get involved with New South to be able to sell food. I got involved with New South to promote organic agriculture and help develop a network of resources and farmers. This network makes it easier for new farmers to come in and certify organic, and have an outlet to sell into."

Tara has a big-picture view of sustainability and organics,

something she often hears from other members of the New South Co-op board. She says that view is what enabled her to be so successful as a member of the board—she was able to see the big picture, not just how the co-op could can benefit her farm, but how the co-op can benefit community and organic agriculture across the state. Tara notes that she could just work her own small farm, but her reach is much smaller individually than if she combines not only with other farmers, but with Heifer USA to further what she calls her "organic agenda."

A COOPERATIVE EFFORT

Unexpectedly, getting involved with the co-op *has* allowed her to sell more. In fact, after adding three high tunnels over the last few years, they've taken their operation from six to twelve months a year. Tara had hoped that spreading out the business over the course of the year would lighten the load in May, June, and July—the traditionally-busy months of the growing season. Instead, it's meant less of a break in the usually-slower winter. But, it's also allowed her to hire a year-round farm hand, Mike—a game changer for a farm their size. Aside from his willingness to work, and work hard, it's a huge load off Tara's plate to not have to train a new hired hand every spring.

> "I fell for organic hard, and I believe in it. I've known since the beginning that if we were going to do this, this is the way I wanted to grow,"

During the first two years of the internship program, Tara says she was really learning alongside her students. Though repetition is a reality of working on a farm, it's important to her that interns experience more than ten weeks of physical labor—she wants to help them learn the *why* behind the work on the farm. Internships and apprenticeships are very common, particularly on small farms, and over the years Tara has noted that many interns are essentially treated as free labor. "I've developed a curriculum for them. I have a series of ten topics that our interns learn about over our ten-week summer internship. Once a week, they actually have a classroom session," she says. While she appreciates the labor help, what she likes even more is that interns bring an energy to the farm that Mike and Tara value. "We're a little older and tired," she says, laughing.

AN ORGANIC LIFE

On a recent road trip to Colorado, Tara and her husband had a conversation about the responses to organic farming from conventional farmers. When she hears conventional farmers say, "Organic can't feed the world," her first response is that conventional farming is not feeding the world. "We have millions and millions of people who are going hungry not for lack of food, but for problems in our policies," she explains.

Her second response is that organic farming will not feed the world if our culture continues to eat the way we do right now, or for that matter, live the way we do right now. Tara points out that in many ways, we live in a society that's very disposable and very fast. "Conventional corn is being used to make plastic. It's being used to make fuel. It's being put to use for purposes that feed into our current lifestyle which is not a sustainable lifestyle," she says. "So, sure," Tara continues, "organic can't feed that lifestyle, that culture."

As Tara and her husband drove through Kansas and Nebraska, they noted the many fields that were planted in corn, most likely for use in plastics or fuel. "What if, Tara asks, just 100 acres of that space were planted in food people could actually eat?" Tara acknowledges the reasoning behind comments that organic farming can't feed the world—primarily, that there isn't enough space to grow crops that aren't modified for high output or disease resistance—but she says it's just the tip of the iceberg of the real issues. "There are so many other issues that have to be solved before we can begin to find out if organic farming can feed the world," she says.

"I was self-taught and it's so hard," Tara explains, "not to mention expensive." If a crop isn't planted at the correct time or in the correct conditions, often the grower must wait until the next year to try again. Tara believes organic farming can feed the world, but she also knows it's going to take a lot of farmers—so while she acknowledges why others worry about competition, she really thinks that what's needed is *more* organic farmers. Tara adds, "The more I can do to make that easier for other people coming in where they don't have some of the same barriers that I had, that's what I want my legacy to be, not just growing tomatoes—although, I'm pretty good at growing tomatoes."

When Tara and her husband originally purchased their property, she fully intended to turn it into a riding arena. She looks out over what are instead vegetable fields , saying, "This is never done. It can just consume you if you let it. And without a doubt, finding balance is hard." She continues, "What I'm hoping is that in five years, we're happy and healthy, and everybody's able to do all this and still loving it. And if not, then that will take a different direction too. But I don't anticipate that. In all of that stuff that I've done, as I've floated, it's never been like this. This is where I've set roots down, literally."

____

Location: Vilonia
Known for: Organic produce
Site: rattlesgarden.com
Social: 🅕 @Rattles-Garden 🅞 @rattlesgarden

SCOTT MCGEHEE

In 2017, Yellow Rocket Concepts, a fast-growing restaurant group that includes Lost Forty Brewing, Zaza Pizza and Salad, Heights Taco & Tamale Co., Local Lime, and Big Orange, purchased about 1.2 million dollars' worth of Arkansas-produced fruits, vegetables, and meats, making them one of the largest purchasers of local meat and produce in the state. Because partner Scott McGehee believes so strongly in the benefits of local food, his goal is to dramatically increase the percentage of what they purchase locally every year. "We're always finding better and newer ways to incorporate more local things into our menus," he says.

Though Scott believes it's the right thing to do, he says there's also a more practical reason to buy local—it's actually less expensive to use local farms. Because the local food movement has made such a public name for itself, that may seem counterintuitive. But, for restaurants purchasing quality produce, a truckload of heirloom tomatoes shipped across the country can be quite expensive. And, regardless of their quality, those tomatoes will not be as fresh and therefore not as delicious as tomatoes grown and picked locally. Scott considers his choice to support local farms to be a lifestyle, saying, "It's critically important for me. Not only do they give me these amazing ingredients to work with, there's just this incredible palette to select from."

Scott was born in Fayetteville while his father was playing for the Razorbacks. When Scott was three years old, his father finished college, and the family returned to Little Rock. Scott's father opened Juanita's, the Little Rock icon, in 1985, and Blue Mesa Grill in 1989. Scott's childhood was focused on food, so it's perhaps little surprise that he packed up and moved to Berkeley, California, after only a couple years in college as a history major. While there, he attended the California Culinary Academy before working for Chef Alice Waters at Chez Panisse from around 1991 to 1997.

After traveling and cooking in Italy, he eventually returned to Little Rock, where he opened Boulevard Bread Company instead of the fine-dining restaurant he originally envisioned. "I was going to do the signature Scott McGehee farm-to-table restaurant," he explains, but says he realized there wasn't anywhere to get great, European-style crusty bread—or good coffee, or cut-to-order cheese.

That led him to realize, "We should open a bakery and a pantry, a gourmet pantry, a provisions kind of place where people in this community can find these things that are so hard to find." This was before Kroger had a significant cheese selection, before Fresh Market and Whole Foods came to Arkansas. This was the late 90s, when the Food Network was becoming very popular, and people were starting to really experiment with cooking. Boulevard Bread Company opened in 1999 and began purchasing organic produce from Sue and Rusty Nuffer, whom Scott says were some of the first organic producers in the state. Today, Boulevard Bread Company—now amicably owned by Christina Basham, Scott's ex-wife and the mother of his two sons—is still one of the largest purchasers of the Nuffer's produce.

Scott says he empathizes with farms and farm families because he knows them, he's developed relationships with them, and he knows how hard it is for them to feed their families and buy gas in the wintertime. He remains cognizant of the fact that for these people and their farms, it's not a get-rich-quick job, he says.

One of the highlights of every week for Scott is going to the farmer's market, where he can interact with farm partners who have become friends. Scott relays the story of going to the market one Saturday morning and seeing a farmer with a huge pile of green garlic. He asked whether any had sold that day. "And the farmer said, 'I have not sold one stalk.' I said, 'Okay, I'll take it all.'" Scott paid a premium for that garlic, no questions asked, and made a great pizza with it. That day, he also found a huge pile of leeks and a massive table of chard—all of which went in the back of his truck.

"They can't afford to grow this stuff and throw it in the trash or in the compost pile," he says. Though he loves swinging by the markets—Hillcrest on Saturdays and The Bernice Garden on Sundays—he holds off on arriving until later in the day, when he tries to pinpoint which items the farmers really need to get rid of. "Out of respect for local people, my guests, my customers, whom I love and cherish, I don't even hit the markets until 10:30."

It's that same respect that resulted in a conscious decision to create restaurants and concepts where guests could feel they were having a $50 or $100 experience but get out the door for $15 if they chose. "I really wanted places that were community inclusive. I want the farmers who sell to me to be able to afford to eat at my restaurants. So, I did not create the signature, Scott McGehee fine-dining restaurant, and I'm really happy that's the direction I took," he says, though he still occasionally prepares a five-course meal with paired wines."

"It's actually less expensive to use local farms."

Scott says he believes Yellow Rocket Concepts does well at balancing affordability for guests, using high quality ingredients, supporting local farms and farm families, and making good, ethical decisions whenever they can. He also believes that the effort is "worth it." But, it's not just about good food and supporting farms. An additional part of their mission, Scott says, is to look at the health of the environment and how their decisions impact that health. They began trying to decrease the use of plastic straws in their restaurants before it became a nationwide movement, and the group is constantly evaluating whether disposable items like to-go containers and cups can be found from more sustainable sources.

To take it a step further, Scott has developed his own sort of community supported agriculture program (CSA). He works with Kelly Carney of North Pulaski Farms to subsidize his tomato crop. If Carney plants 100 rows of tomatoes, Scott will pay for the costs of a predetermined number of rows—the plants, the shade cloth, Carney's labor, everything. The kicker for Carney is, Scott covers those costs in the winter, allowing Carney to earn income during the slim months. Then, when the crop comes in, the tomatoes belong to Scott. If it's a good year, he ends up paying less for tomatoes than everyone else—but if it's a bad year, or a blight comes, he loses money.

Scott doesn't mind taking the risk along with his farm partners. He says, "Ultimately, it's great for them, because it's money they can depend on every year, and it's money they receive when it's needed most—when the growing season's not happening. It's kind of a new way of doing business, but it's very supportive of them. It makes me feel good that I'm taking the risk with them, because farming is a very risky business."

He continues, "A late frost, a hail storm, can absolutely demolish you. The government doesn't sweep in for every little hail storm. They have no problem bailing out giant conglomerate farms, but the small farmer's pretty much out there on an island."

Scott's first experience growing was in the garden with his great-grandparents. His great-grandmother, Ruby Thomas, and great-grandfather, Herbert L. Thomas, founded the Red Apple Inn in 1963 and owned it until the early 80s. Ruby was the genius in the kitchen, in the restaurant, and with the decor. Scott's great-aunt opened the first restaurant in Little Rock's Hillcrest neighborhood, The Copper Kettle. In her home kitchen, Scott says the main dish served was a vegetable plate that utilized preserved food, mushrooms, bacon, grains, and lots of sweet potatoes in the winter and thick-sliced tomatoes, greens, corn on the cob, ponebread, field peas, and beans in the summer. As an ode to his great-grandmother, Scott says his "retirement restaurant" would probably be full of Arkansas country cooking—very simple food. "My idea is to have 30 rotating vegetables that are just prepared beautifully and simply," he says.

Right: Scott McGehee prepares squash in his home kitchen.

——

Location: Little Rock
Known for: Concept restaurants focused on cuisine made accessible
Social: @scottychef

LOBLOLLY CREAMERY

After moving into her home near Little Rock's South Main neighborhood, Sally Mengel repainted the exterior a mint-green color—after all, she is in the ice cream business. She laughed infectiously as she peered up at the paint and commented, "It is really bright, isn't it?"

Sally, an only child, grew up mostly in Boston and St. Louis. Her father liked to move every few years for work, and so she was exposed to the local cultures of several regions of the United States.

Of herself as a child, Sally says, "I was shy, quiet. I remember in middle school, my class had a debate. My side was why you should drink soy milk. In doing dairy research, I got my family to switch to soy milk, so dairy's always been in my life. I was really into art. I didn't know what graphic design was, but I liked playing with Paint and Publisher, making ads. I liked to take summer art classes."

By the time she graduated from Emory University in 2009, her parents had moved to Little Rock, and Sally followed, her move to Little Rock also constituting the first visit she'd ever made to the city.

In college, she studied global health and anthropology, thinking she wanted to work in public health, a logical track given that both her parents are physicians. But her real passion was, and still is, food—particularly sustainable food systems. "I took an anthropology class on food systems and their complications. During my sophomore year of college, Emory started a sustainability office. One of their programs offered grants for student projects, like starting a farmer's market or maybe ecological projects. I noticed the coffee on campus sucked."

Sally also realized there was no opportunity to work on campus except jobs related to students' financial aid packages. There was a disconnect between students who did and didn't work. And since coffee is, as Sally says, basically the number one commodity on college campuses, she applied for and received a student grant to open a coffee cart, pioneering fair trade coffee on campus. "We started this student-run coffee cart called the Green Bean. That's what I really got into and loved. I focused on that more than

college," Sally says, "and it got me inspired about where food comes from, sourcing, sustainability, entrepreneurship, small business—all that stuff." The coffee cart still exists today as a kiosk in the food court at Emory.

When Sally first came to Little Rock, ice cream wasn't exactly on her radar. It was difficult for a new college graduate with such specific interests to get a job in Little Rock, so she worked with Literacy Action— a local nonprofit that helps adults learn to read—and as a house sitter. However, it wasn't long before she got involved with Village Commons, a nonprofit that pursues projects related to community, environment, and urban gardening. She began working with the Arkansas Sustainability Network, now the Arkansas Local Food Network, facilitating pickups on Saturdays. "I was really intrigued by local foods and the farmer's markets and all that. The Root Café was doing events before they opened a restaurant," she says.

Village Commons was next door to The Green Corner Store, both of which opened in 2009. In 2010, Sally began working at The Green Corner Store as a clerk. "South Main was a thriving community in the early 1900s through the 1960s, but it was just rehabilitating after the tornado of 1999. There are—were—a lot of empty buildings." At the time, according to Sally, there wasn't a lot of public funding going into the area, but local resident Anita Davis began purchasing and rehabilitating buildings in South Main.

In 2011, Anita purchased the original vintage fixtures of the Lincoln Building, in which The Green Corner Store is housed. The building was erected for Dawson's Drug Store, which was a pharmacy and soda fountain from 1906–1967. "Supposedly it was the last pharmacy in Arkansas to have a pharmacy license, a liquor license, and a gun license, so you could buy guns, liquor, and drugs!" Sally quickly ticks these three items off on her right hand, ending her explanation with, "That's what I always tell people."

Sally envisioned something small and manageable where she would simply make ice cream and sell it from the Green Corner Store. She would also offer homemade syrups for handcrafted sodas, and maybe some old-fashioned beverages like egg creams, phosphates, and malts. Taking its name from the state tree of Arkansas, Loblolly Creamery premiered in November of 2011 at the first annual Cornbread Festival. Sally purchased Loblolly's first ice cream machine the day before. Until that point, Sally and cofounder Rachel Moore had been experimenting with recipes using their home machine, but they had never used a commercial one.

"The ice cream turned out super icy, chunky, and gross and I was like, 'Oh my god, we can't do this.' But we served it anyway." Loblolly entered a caramel polenta corn cake with a scoop of buttermilk and berry compote in the festival's non-traditional category—and won. "That gave me a boost of confidence," Sally remembers.

After their debut, Loblolly worked to open a soda fountain in The Green Corner Store. At first, there was just a single small freezer in the store, and the ice cream was made at Trinity Episcopal Church. The church wasn't using their cafeteria kitchen, so they rented it out to Loblolly, Kent Walker Cheese, Sharea Soup, and A Pie Lady. (Trinity Episcopal is also where The Root Café prepared food for catering events during fundraising for the restaurant.)

Sally takes a deep breath, thinking back to the beginning when Loblolly had a small staff of three. She continues, "We opened April 1 of 2012. It was just me and Rachel, and we hired her brother Dan. They made ice cream and I worked the soda fountain. The three of us did everything."

Slowly, friends of Loblolly who worked at local restaurants began requesting their ice cream. Their restaurant reach grew longer, and they also began sampling at events. Soon, they were selling at Hillcrest Farmer's Market. Before long, people were asking how they could find Loblolly at grocery stores, and Sally's original vision for Loblolly evolved: "We thought it was going to be small, but then it kind of snowballed into an ice cream manufacturing business where we made bulk ice cream in custom flavors for restaurants and cafés, doing catering. We ended up getting an ice cream truck." That truck is now well-recognized around town for its lively mint green paint, fun font, and the solar panels that provide much of the necessary power.

In the summer of 2017, Loblolly moved out of The Green Corner Store and into the space next door that formerly housed Village Commons. Sally says sharing space had been nice, but the soda fountain had limited hours and square footage, which limited the menu. While the previous space could only hold eight flavors, the new scoop shop keeps thirty-two flavors at all times.

"A couple of years ago, I wouldn't have been sure about opening an independent scoop shop, but I think now, with a lot more late-night restaurants, it's really time to develop the Loblolly experience," she says. Much of the Loblolly experience includes educating consumers about what it is Loblolly does.

"It's been really great having relationships with the people who grow produce we use in the ice cream. Having relationships means they'll let us know when things are ready and in season. Because fruit does not have to look perfect for ice cream, we get great deals from local farmers and we provide them with another avenue for imperfect fruit." Though it may sound like a win-win—and indeed it is—Loblolly had to establish themselves as a business before developing those relationships. If they'd placed orders they were unable to finalize, local producers would have lost faith in Loblolly's ability to follow through. It's one thing for a company to place an order with a large national supplier and not follow through; backing out on an order with a small local producer directly impacts that producer's bottom line.

Local producers well know the name of the game when it comes to seasonality and the complexities of food production. What's been more difficult, Sally says, is educating consumers about seasonality. She says, "People want strawberry ice cream all year round, but I don't want to make ice cream in which the strawberries are from out of country. It's also a sustainability issue regarding the carbon use. But farmers now are starting to freeze items so we can get them out of season, to a degree." Preservation allows Loblolly to increase the length of time certain flavors are available each year.

Sally acknowledges that it isn't just consumers who need educating—sometimes it's Sally herself. She says, "It was hard

to source some things in the beginning, because I assumed they would be available longer than they actually are, or it was unexpected when the season actually was. Barnhill has strawberries at the end of February, which is super early. But some years it may be March or April, so it's important to be flexible."

That flexibility is useful when experimenting with flavors. It's not always expected, what works—persimmon was a no-go, but purple sweet potato ice cream is a popular October flavor. When the crop doesn't yield, or for some reason there's been a shortage, it can be tough on Loblolly, but they've learned to be flexible.

"I think it's more fun to get a challenge, like acorn flour. We've done a lot of flavors I probably wouldn't do again, but they were fun to try. We made a local garlic ice cream. I probably wouldn't do that again either," she says. Each batch is only about three gallons, so a failed experiment isn't too costly.

"Whole Foods gave us the opportunity to come in and so we've learned a lot about SKUs (Stock Keeping Units) and product lines. We call them our signature flavors—flavors we can provide all year long. Every four months we have a new seasonal line, and we're also getting known for custom flavors. It gives us huge flexibility to use whatever's in season."

Sally pauses for a moment to reply to her baker, who's just sent her a text. Her eyes widen. "Oh my goodness," Sally says. "She's making donuts."

When asked whether she still enjoys ice cream, she answers immediately, with no thought necessary: "I love ice cream. I'll eat it from Sonic; I'll eat it from a high-end restaurant; I'll eat it from Loblolly. I'm going to New York this weekend, and I have ten places I want to try. And we *are* going to go to all of them." It's not simply a sweet tooth that spurs her enjoyment. Early on in her ice cream career, she and her team attended an ice cream short course at Pennsylvania State University.

Many of the other students were from large corporations; thus, she was able to see how different Loblolly really was. But ice cream school also taught her how to appreciate the nuances of her craft. Now, she's something of an ice cream sommelier. For example, spicy ice cream is a delayed spicy—it develops in the back of your throat. She asks, "How does the flavor bloom? How do you layer flavors? How does it melt? What's the texture?"

A couple of years ago, Loblolly diversified their menu. They already sold brownies and cookies to accompany sundaes and ice cream sandwiches, and so adding other types of goodies, like macarons, was a logical addition. The baked goods sell well and help stabilize sales in the winter when ice cream isn't as popular. "The foundation of the business is trying to make everything from scratch—not only our ice cream but marshmallows, waffle cone batter, maraschino cherries, hot fudge, brownies, and macarons. Making most everything from scratch is really our big mission."

Small-batch ice cream isn't cheap, and Loblolly uses the best ingredients they can. Sally points out that many people frequent coffee shops, often spending $7 or more on a single beverage and don't think twice about it, yet they are sometimes surprised at the cost of a pint of Loblolly. "I try to keep our price point pretty low, like at least one thing on the menu that's just two dollars, so people can afford a treat." She points out that though ice cream is, in fact, a treat, as opposed to a dietary staple, it's an indulgence she wants everyone to have access to.

———

Location: Little Rock
Known for: Handmade everything
Site: loblollycreamery.com
Social: @LoblollyCreamery @weloveloblolly
@loblollycreamery

ANITA DAVIS

"As you age, and you're looking at your life, if there are things you can do [to improve the world] that're in line with your philosophy, I think you have an obligation to do those things."

Anita Davis says she hasn't always been so passionate about making a difference in her community. "I've always cared, but I never really felt I could make a difference." Instead, she says, all her projects now are things she was really interested in. "I want the earth to make it. I want women to be heard, have a voice, and understand what our mothers went through." Those interests evolved into the advocacy she now so eloquently expresses.

In 2005, Anita purchased a parking lot on South Main Street where a chain fish restaurant had burned down. The site has been transformed into The Bernice Garden, which was officially founded in 2007. It began as a simple seating area with minimal landscaping. Today, an open-air canopy feeds rainfall into a cistern which waters the ample green life throughout the space.

When Anita bought the property, she was learning the role plants and greenery play in absorbing rainfall so that storm drains don't become overwhelmed. She was also coming to understand how vital plants are to mitigating flooding concerns.

Though the garden has continued to evolve, it currently hosts a Sunday farmers market and a revolving art exhibition. It is intended to be a space not just for enjoyment, but for the community to gather. "I wanted it to feel sacred," she says.

When The Bernice Garden Farmers' Market opened, the slow food movement—which promotes traditional cooking, local food, and the role of farmers—had already started. Still, Anita says, she wanted to contribute for personal reasons as well. "It seemed important to me to have a farmers market, because I grew up in the 50s. We all had a lot of vegetables in small towns, with gardens in the backyard. There were always people with peas on the back of their trucks during pea season. Everyone would freeze or can all those wonderful foods."

Those memories are part of what pushed Anita to participate in the creation of The Cornbread Festival, where professional and amateur chefs serve their version of cornbread and a side dish for judging by the public and a panel of judges. The festival, which began in 2012, has become a much-anticipated annual event on South Main. "It felt," Anita says, "like the festival could be a way to teach people ways to introduce more vegetables into their diets. I'm such a believer in eating well." It's partly for that reason that The Bernice Garden Farmers' Market accepts SNAP benefits. She is aware of a number of people in the SoMa neighborhood of Little Rock, where the Garden is located, that can use help buying produce, particularly the more expensive organic produce The Bernice Garden Farmers' Market is known for. "It's important for everyone to have that opportunity," Anita says.

Anita grew up in Murfreesboro, but, armed with a home economics degree, she moved to Little Rock when her husband was in pharmacy school and began working for the Arkansas Dairy Council. She says the nutrition part of that position was what interested her the most. When asked why she was so excited for The Root Café to open in the old Sweden Cream building, her excitement was evident when she responded, "We had to. We just had to!" Because there wasn't a lot of farm to table at the time, she says it was a priority to find a restaurant for the space that could fill that need.

Today, Anita spends many of her days working in ESSE Museum & Store, just down the street from the garden, where she curates exhibits designed to tell the stories of "our mothers and grandmothers." The museum is the only purse museum in the entire country, and one of just three in the world. Though Anita says she's likely to start trying to relax a little more, she responds, "Who knows?" to the question of what the future will bring. "My life has been backward. I was able to travel early on in life, and then had a nice opportunity to stay home with my children. I always had an entrepreneurial bent, but this is the longest I've worked on one project—I think because it's heart-based."

————

Location: Little Rock
Known as: The godmother of South Main
Site: thebernicegarden.org
Social: 🅕@TheBerniceGarden 🅣@BerniceGarden

HEIFER INTERNATIONAL

"I wish more people knew that Heifer International is more than just the gift catalogue," says Ardyth Neill, president of the nonprofit foundation headquartered in downtown Little Rock. The slim, glossy gift catalogue she's referring to is sent to previous donors and others each holiday season—a colorful reminder that it's time to think about giving, and especially that we have the opportunity and power to share gifts with meaning.

From within its pages, givers can select from bees, ducks, goats, pigs, chickens, dairy and beef cattle, and even llamas to be given to a family in need somewhere around the world. Those gifts keep on giving. In the case of most animals, the first female offspring is passed to another family, and families often share the knowledge they've gained in animal husbandry with others. Heifer's goal isn't to provide ongoing support to families and communities; instead, it's to increase sustainability and self-reliance among those who receive Heifer gifts. And the focus isn't just on the people—Heifer offers training to recipient farmers so they may learn how to best manage their resources, and those farmers often go on to help train other gift recipients in their communities.

Beyond animals and crop management, Heifer also prides itself on working to increase gender equity, improve the environment, and encourage full participation in community decision making. Heifer's Programs serve nearly one million families in Africa, Asia, and the Americas.

Heifer International is well-known for its work around the globe, but what some don't know is that the organization does much for small-scale farmers right here in Arkansas. Efforts include seed funding for new farm-related businesses, as well as educational opportunities. Every year, the 1,200-acre Heifer Ranch in Perryville, about an hour northwest of Little Rock, hosts dozens of school field trips and a number of free workshops for local farmers, including On-Farm Poultry Processing, Lambing Production, Food Safety Practices for Small to Mid-Scale Producers, How Farm Credit Administration Works with Arkansas Farmers, and Backyard Chickens 101. Overnight visits, individual tours, and service-learning classes are also popular. Available for sale from the Ranch is pasture-raised meat and vegetables, all grown by Heifer-affiliated farmers.

Heifer Ranch has been the start of a number of Little Rock foodies' journeys, including that of Jack Sundell from The Root Café, (see page 17), and it was at Heifer Ranch that two Arkansas-based farmer co-ops got their start: Grass Roots Cooperative and New South Cooperative (see next page).

———

Location: Worldwide, Headquartered in Little Rock
Known for: Giving a hand up to people around the world
Site: heifer.org
Social: ⓕ@heiferinternational ⓧ@heifer

CO-OPS

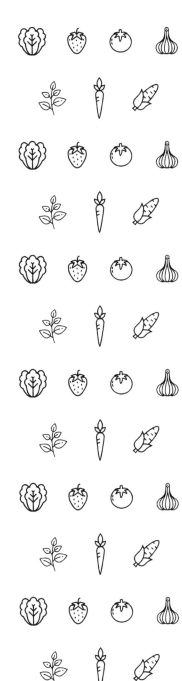

CENTRAL ARKANSAS COOPERATIVES

Cooperatives have long been a popular form of sub-versive economic structure, but it's only been in the last few years that two have gained name recognition among the residents of Central Arkansas. Both were seeded by Heifer International, a worldwide non-profit based in Little Rock, and both have gone on to do work at the state level in an effort to create a cooperative structure that benefits both the farmers and the consumers.

NEW SOUTH COOPERATIVE

These progressive farmers are working together to support each other and provide tastier and fresher produce to the community. They have pooled their resources to purchase trucks and trailers, which can be parked and loaded in different regions of Arkansas and Western Tennessee since farms are so spread out across the state. Farmers will drop their product in the cooled trailers, and trucks can pick up different trailers cutting down on fuel costs, a major expense. The cooperative runs a yearly CSA pickup available through spring, summer, and fall, as well as year-round wholesale to local restaurants, grocers and institutions.

GRASS ROOTS COOPERATIVE

Grass Roots Cooperative is a farmer-owned coop-erative that focuses on producing high-quality meat raised and processed in small batches. Grass-fed, hormone free, and non-GMO is the rule, not the exception. Each label includes information on who raised the meat, where they raised it, and when it was processed. Grass Roots ships across Arkansas, and in some areas, a regularly-scheduled pickup can be added to weekly CSA pickups from New South Cooperative.

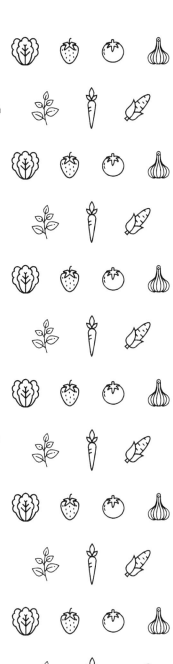

JOSH HARDIN

At only thirty-eight years old, Josh Hardin is one of the most respected growers in Arkansas. Josh and his wife Anna, a dietician, own forty acres in Sheridan which they have turned into the Laughing Stock Farm, the name coming from other farmers' collective opinion of Josh when he forewent conventional chemical fertilizers and began organic farming.

Farming comes naturally to Josh. A fifth-generation Delta farmer, Josh grew up on his family's 1,000-acre farm in Grady. He was vice president of the Pine Bluff Farmers Market at only fourteen years old and was driving produce before he even had a driver's license.

Growing up on a commercial farm honed Josh's growing skills, teaching him the basics of planting and cultivating, but he also developed his own system of beliefs surrounding commercial farming. He came by this honestly. His great uncle Joe, a legislator who was on the original Board of Directors of the Arkansas Farm Bureau, was one of the first sustainable rice farmers in Arkansas. Joe Hardin, a family legend, brought koi fish in from Japan and let them loose in the rice paddies, a practice that some believe reduces the need for fertilizer and has the added benefit of raising two commodities, rice and koi, on one plot of land.

Similar to his uncle, Josh is a conservationist. He grew frustrated by the chemicals "flying overhead daily" to dump pesticides on neighboring crops when he was growing organic produce on the family land. Josh faced the additional challenge of finding the demand for his produce locally.

His family farm was sending sweet corn and watermelons north. Their main customers were in Michigan and Minnesota, and Josh was worried that his home state was not only losing its fresh vegetables but giving away its valuable natural resources in the soil as well.

"I love Little Rock because it is a microcosm of eaters and foodies. I want to immerse myself in that, but it's not enough. Every farm I know in that top tier is shipping ninety percent of their product out of Arkansas. They can't grow that kind of stuff, and they will pay double. They value our food more than we do. I mean, we love watermelons. We love corn, but we don't eat very much of it. We eat it at a picnic," Josh says.

Hoping to encourage Arkansas residents to consume their own food, Josh's older half-brother Jody introduced him to the River Market Farmers' Market in Little Rock where he could sell his organic produce. The brothers opened Hardin's River Mercantile in 2006 and began selling baskets of local produce from across the state. This was basically the beginning of Community Supported Agriculture (CSA) boxes in Central Arkansas and would later develop into Hardin's co-op, New South Cooperative—a group of local farmers certified organic or naturally grown who share equipment and work together to provide local produce to the community.

It was at the River Market where Josh met Sue and Rusty Nuffer of Armstead Mountain Farms. The couple would greatly influence Josh as an organic farmer.

"They were the grandparents of organic in Arkansas and my inspiration. They were at the River Market, and they would be in the very back of the market, the very back corner, this obscure little thing, and they'd be sold out by nine a.m.," laughs Josh. "They were just doing it right. They had pictures and recipes. Back then, they were the only ones doing this."

The Nuffers had left corporate jobs out of state and moved back to the land and organic farming. They told Josh about a program at the University of California at Santa Cruz that offered apprenticeships in agroecology and sustainable food systems. The six-month training taught Josh about soil management, crop rotation, organic growing, and natural pest control. This widely-recognized program has educated many of Arkansas's organic growers. Josh learned invaluable lessons through the experience and connected with growers around the country. He came back to Arkansas with a stronger desire to make his philosophy around food and the environment meet the necessity of paying the bills.

"People look at farmers and think, 'Oh, you're just okay being broke,'" Josh says. "It is an incredibly broke profession. I get why the stereotype is there; it's very real. I've never been okay with that. I became a farmer not to be broke but to have control of my destiny and my income."

Josh and Anna both believe that fresh, diverse, organic food is imperative not only to their own health but to the health of a

regional community's food and soil system.

"In a way, we are on this mission to get people to eat more healthy food and teach them the alternatives," Josh says. "We are still Southern; we eat Southern-style foods, too, but we balance them a lot."

When Josh and Anna purchased what is now Laughing Stock Farm, the property had offers already extended, but the sellers believed in the Hardins and wanted to support them.

The selling feature of the property was a large lake—a promising water source. The property collects rainwater, lake water, city water, and well water. "Water rich" is the term Josh uses to describe his farm. Josh laughs, "If I learned anything from California, it's to have water."

Another bonus was that much of the property was surrounded by woods, creating a natural barrier to neighboring farms' fertilizers. Josh knew his neighbors wouldn't necessarily be concerned about his organic crops, so he needed to invest in a barrier as part of the property. Most of the land in the county is timber land, another encouraging sign, since timber companies rarely spray chemicals.

Josh grows all kinds of vegetables but has developed a knack for more exotic plants like ginger and turmeric. He grows lettuce, onions, garlic, tomatoes, and peppers but likes to

diversify his crops to maintain soil health. He now sells through New South Cooperative and at The Bernice Garden Farmers' Market (see Anita Davis, page 35). Family dinners feature food fresh from the garden, and Josh and Anna's dreams of instilling an appreciation for food culture in their children is coming true. But farming is not a nine-to-five job, and Josh admits it can be difficult, as he now holds a full-time position. Still, it's important to the family that they cook a healthy meal and get everyone together at the table.

"My goal in life is to just be valued somewhere, to have something not everybody else has," says Josh. "All these years of struggling and failing have been worth it because people really appreciate those experiences. If you've failed and overcome it, that makes a good story. That makes a good teacher. Believe me, I've tried it all."

His expertise has been hugely beneficial to the New South Cooperative (see page 37). As well as mentoring new farmers, Josh formed relationships with Scott McGehee of Yellow Rocket Concepts (see page 26) and several other local chefs, which he brought to the co-op. These chefs now use New South for produce and benefit from a group of farms instead of relying on an individual farm to source produce. The name "New" South even hints at this group's way of thinking.

"The old guard is on its way out," Josh says. "I see an opportunity for the young, sustainable-minded progressive folks to get in and take the reins."

All members in New South are required to be certified organic or naturally grown, and Josh says everyone brings something to the table, be it experience, contacts, resources, or ideas. The co-op helps these farmers weather bad years—Josh often references the unpredictability of Arkansas weather—and provide more variety to customers.

"Our products change because our consumers change," Josh notes. "We always want something different. We are constantly watching what's new on the Food Channel, Instagram, or with the latest chef."

> # "All these years of struggling and failing have been worth it because people really appreciate those experiences. If you've failed and overcome it, that makes a good story. That makes a good teacher."

Josh's crops will surely look different in the coming years. Josh sees great potential in industrial hemp. His fascination with growing hemp in Arkansas goes back to his teenage years, when he and some friends stumbled upon a University of Georgia test plot in Grady. Driving some back roads, Josh and his buddies couldn't believe their luck when they found twelve-foot-high plants that they thought were cannabis.

"We just happened to to drive by," says Josh. "Of course, a bunch of punk kids, we said, 'Cut it down! Fill the truck up!' Then we got home and there was nothing that looked remotely like cannabis."

Fascinated by the plant, *Cannabis sativa*—varieties of which produce both hemp and marijuana— Josh went on to conduct his science fair project on the hemp test plot. The plant he had mistaken for marijuana was actually its taller, thinner alter ego, hemp, which lacks the high THC content of marijuana but can be used for fibers in clothing, paper, and textiles. Speaking with the growers, Josh was shocked to learn the hemp had grown and flourished in an unirrigated and unfertilized field during one of the worst drought years, right in his hometown.

This experience would become the background for Josh's adventurous new role as Director of Cultivation and Indigenous Education for One World Pharma, which has provided his most challenging farming plot yet: eighty acres in Popayan, Colombia. Having consulted on this project for years, Josh has temporarily relocated to Colombia to focus on growing hemp and cannabis to extract CBD and THC for pharmaceutical purposes.

"This job is wild. There is never a dull moment," says Josh. "I miss the security and sanity, but I'm taking all of my knowledge and experience. This is the tropics. It's grow time 365 days a year."

Every thirty days, Josh returns to Arkansas to visit his family for a week. Being away is difficult, to say the least, but the opportunity to grow a one-hundred-percent-organic product and be on the cutting edge of this industry is one Josh couldn't forego.

Josh hopes Arkansas will become a big player in this industry. He stays on top of the legislation and is a vocal advocate for progressive policies in farming. It's clear that not only has Josh developed his sustainable way of thinking from his Uncle Joe but also his passion for the legislative side of farming.

"I've watched friends die on prescription drugs. I want to be part of the solution. I've always believed food is medicine, but I now think it's the plants that are the medicine."

———

Location: Sheridan
Known as: A revolutionary in the local food movement

Most Arkansans would not draw a natural connection between their state and a Mediterranean culture, but in terms of food, Mylo Coffee's owner Stephanos Mylonas believes there are many similarities.

Stephanos was born and raised in Cyprus, an island in the eastern Mediterranean Sea, just off the southern coast of Turkey and the western coasts of Syria and Lebanon. Growing up, Stephanos was exposed to fresh, local food as a way of life. Since Cyprus is an island, residents grew their own food because it was more economical, as well as flavorful.

"Little Rock and Cyprus have similar latitudes. We grew tomatoes, okra, watermelons, strawberries, eggplant, and purple peas. If you think about Greek food, there is a strong relation there."

Stephanos's focus on food and its preparation sets his coffee shop apart from its competitors. At Mylo, in Little Rock's Hillcrest neighborhood, you can have a made-to-order breakfast like a bacon, egg, and halloumi (a type of cheese made from goat and sheep milk) sandwich or house-made ricotta toast along with an assortment of fresh, daily baked goods, which take up a counter space the entire width of the store. Mylo also offers lunch with a daily soup or stew special and a selection of homemade sandwiches with several vegetarian options.

Having developed a love of baking from his mother and grandmother, Stephanos started serving his baked goods at his first business, a late-night music venue in Bristol, England. He would work late into the night and, a naturally industrious person, would wake before most of his friends with his mornings free. He started baking and would take his creations to the music venue's staff. They were well received, so he added a catering service to his business. It became quite popular, and large organizations in the UK—including Aardman Animations, the creators of *Wallace and Gromit*—would host functions at Stephanos's venue.

One specialty treat that Stephanos brought with him to the US is the kouign amman. Made of laminated dough like a croissant (Mylo has a large lamination machine in the back of the shop), the kouign amman is denser and sweeter than a croissant. The kouign amman, which regularly comes in chocolate, poached pear, or original, is known as one of the more difficult pastries to make, and Mylo almost always runs out by the end of the day.

At Mylo, the motto is: if it can be made, we will make it in-house. Everything from jams and preserves used as spreads, to bottled teas and lemonades, to the mochi donuts (a gluten free donut made with a Japanese rice flour in place of yeast), and pie crust for quiches are homemade. Stephanos even makes his sandwich pickles from local cucumbers. Although a much more time-consuming and not necessarily a cost-effective way to operate, this is the only way Stephanos knows. He believes that he is making a long-term investment in his product. Over time, the process will become more efficient, and he will have an edge over his competitors. He also believes it is his duty to provide food of the highest quality to paying customers.

"Every single croissant, koiugn amman, and hand pie was produced by me," Stephanos claims. "Not because I don't trust anyone else, but because it is a process that must be done separately from the kitchen, and it is the process that I most enjoy. You would be surprised how many restaurants charge you a premium for something they didn't make."

When Stephanos followed love to Little Rock and sold his interest in his UK business, he knew he wanted to start something that combined his passions for business and for food. Mylo Coffee emerged initially as a stand at Hillcrest Farmers' Market in the summer of 2012.

"I'm very proud to say that, for me, it was a very conscious decision to start forming relationships at the Farmers' Market," Stephanos states. It allowed him to meet local growers, test their products, and form long-lasting relationships with farmers.

"I know them personally, and they know me personally," Stephanos says. "They will text me pictures or lists of what they have, and this is key because a restaurant owner is always on the fly. I can't check email while I am watching an oven."

This practical and thoughtful way of doing business helps Stephanos maintain efficiency and prepare his menu around what is available. Sometimes an unpredictable weather event can wipe out a local grower's supply of spring mix, for example, and then Stephanos has to make a last-minute trip next door to Kroger to replace his supply. He has learned to adapt and admits that using local ingredients is not always easy, and not always best in some cases.

Being efficient is imperative. If you step behind the counter at Mylo, you will be amazed to see this efficiency in action throughout the kitchen. In what is surely one of the cleanest workspaces in town, there is not a crumb on the floor, every container is clearly labeled and dated, and every surface is wiped to a sparkling perfection. Transparency is evident to customers, who can watch employees scooping ginger molasses cookies when they order or peer through the wall of repurposed antique windows to watch Stephanos use the lamination machine.

As everything is done intentionally at Mylo, this is also intentional.

"You don't have to make a mess," claims Stephanos. "I am not from a culinary school background, but it is something I recognized early on, that if you do something right and keep a clean station, then that is the most efficient way."

Stephanos's brother Markos has also clearly learned this habit from his brother as he creates perfect stacks of coffee labels for the bagged coffee. They share a laugh, though, when talking about first acquiring the roastery space located about a mile up the road. "It looked like an atomic bomb went off in there," Stephanos claims.

Markos is taking the same thoughtful approach to coffee as his brother takes to food. The roastery is Markos's space and his domain, where he hand builds benches and engineers a traveling coffee cart from plans he found online. Markos

started out by wandering through grocery stores smelling coffees before spending years in his own, self-taught version of coffee school.

"In the beginning, it all tastes the same," says Markos. "And then you start smelling different things and tasting different flavors."

Markos purchases high-quality, green coffee from a distributor and roasts it according to his specifications. Markos's roaster uses an infrared flame, as opposed to an open flame, which he believes allows him to control the heat and temperature more effectively, giving him a cleaner roast without a burned taste. The coffee, single origin Brazilian and Guatemalan varieties and a blended espresso, is available for purchase in the store and online. They are already shipping as far as Alaska and hope to partner with local businesses first.

"We want to grow slowly so we can manage it ourselves," says Stephanos. Like their food, the brothers plan to offer a high-quality experience through their coffee. "We hope to encourage customers to think about the flavor profile of the coffee. It should be savored like wine. Sometimes, the food can be a catalyst and sometimes it can hold you back," explains Stephanos.

Really, the entire Mylo experience is about more than just savoring the food or the coffee. It is about slowing down and savoring the moment as well.

———

Location: Little Rock
Known for: Specialty pastries and gourmet coffee
Site: mylocoffee.com
Social: 🌐🐦📷@MyloCoffeeCo

IZARD CHOCOLATE

Located on a quiet street next to Kroger in Little Rock's Hillcrest neighborhood, just around the corner from Mylo Coffee Co. (see page 43), Izard Chocolates was one of the capital city's most unique tourist destinations before its May 2019 closing. Its loss is being felt by many, but its story lives on.

Izard quickly gained a reputation as one of the South's finest artisanal chocolate makers after being featured in several local and national publications (including *Garden & Gun* magazine, which named them one of five "loved" Southern chocolate shops.)

For you who dream of dropping everything and starting a small business, particularly one involving sweets, Izard's founder, Nathaniel Izard, is an inspiration. His tale is also an enlightening lesson on the time and energy it takes to start a small business. One of Little Rock's youngest entrepreneurs, Nathaniel left his sales job at a lighting company to start Izard Chocolates at the age of twenty-two.

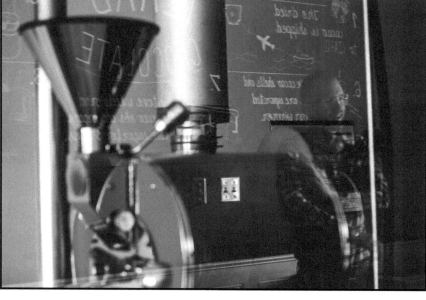

"I didn't want to sit at a desk all day," Nathaniel recounts. "I planned to travel Europe for a year, but my visa ran out after three months. I spent the entire three months in Italy with a family who had a vineyard and made their own wine. When I got back, I told myself I would start a company."

With a passion for baking and specialty products, Nathaniel hoped to become a craftsman. He created a list of potential

products, which included—among other artisanal foods— wine, beer, cheese, and chocolate. He had never made chocolate, so he started where many of us begin, with Google. This is where he became highly intrigued by the chocolate-making process, from the bean to the bar. The process was detailed on a large wall chalkboard at the store's entry.

"You can't go to the grocery store and get the ingredients to make chocolate," Nathaniel muses. "I found this astounding. Chocolate is something we eat all the time. How do so few of us know where it comes from or how it's made?"

The first word Nathaniel learned was *cacao*. Cacao is short for a type of tree, the *Theobroma cacao*, that grows in equatorial countries. It prefers low altitude, rainforest-type environments with heavy humidity. Cacao fruit grows on the trees, and it is a gourd-shaped, pulpy, white fruit, full of seeds. The fruit is harvested and then fermented to bring out the flavor.

"People started throwing this 'cacao' word around, and I was like 'cocoa?'" Nathaniel recalls. "Then, I learned about the cacao fruit. So when you eat chocolate, you are really eating fruit. It's healthy," Nathaniel laughs.

The cacao seeds were removed, dried, and sorted before they finally shipped to Nathaniel, who roasted the seeds in a gleaming red roaster in the front of the store. The earthy, coffee scent would envelop the entire building. The roasting process gives the cacao its flavor. This is one way artisanal chocolates differentiate themselves from large-scale chocolate producers like Hershey's or Mars, by taking more care and time in the roasting process.

Nathaniel sampled cacao from all over the world (not a bad job) and then chose the providers he wished to use. He prided himself on buying only organic, high-quality cacao, and he usually paid much higher than fair-trade standards required.

"We were not trying to be a Hershey's bar," says Nathaniel. "That wasn't our target audience."

Using only cacao and sugar, Izard featured single-origin chocolate bars made from cacao beans from Haiti, Guatemala, and the Dominican Republic. Using beans from just the one country allows the consumer to taste the varying flavors of beans from different regions. The Guatemala bar had a nutty, fudgy flavor with a hint of banana while the Haiti bar was more earthy and subtle. Part of the fun was tasting the chocolate from different regions to recognize which flavors suit your palate.

Single-origin is a term most commonly used in coffee and chocolate to describe beans from a single geographic region, such as a country, farm, or cooperative. Since the beans are sourced from one area only, the consumer can develop an understanding of the tastes specific to that region. Do you prefer beans from a mountainous region or a hotter climate? Does the soil provide a richer, earthier note or a sweeter, berry flavor? Each bean reflects the place where it is grown.

Most store-bought coffees combine beans from different regions into a blend, which has been tested and developed into a consistent taste. Single-origin coffee is usually more expensive, often because it is seasonal, and blends can be produced year-round. Single-origin coffee is often consumed black to highlight the flavor profile and is intended for sipping and enjoying.

Izard also sold flavored bars, which were extremely popular with customers. The Icelandic Sea Salt, Coffee, and Almond bars were composed of a custom blend of cacao beans created by Nathaniel. His salted caramels, chocolate dipped caramels (in flavors like bourbon pecan, raspberry, and chai), and truffles were also hits with customers. These made popular gifts during the holiday season.

"I learned about the cacao fruit. When you eat chocolate, you are really eating fruit. It's healthy."

Nathaniel was always on hand and eager to show visitors around the facility. His smiling face and signature red hair and beard were as recognizable as his chocolates.

Izard was "big on samples," Nathaniel notes. "That's one part of the business I really enjoyed. I didn't think about the relationships I would build with my customers. It's fun to have those close, personal connections."

Nathaniel enjoyed educating his customers on chocolate-making and explaining his tools used in the process. Following the roasting process, Nathaniel transferred the cacao seeds to a homemade winnower that removed the cacao nibs from the shells. Nathaniel's winnower used a Shop-Vac and PVC pipe to suck the shells into a bucket and separate the cacao nibs.

"Most machines used in chocolate making start at $20,000 to $30,000, and the winnower is all about physics, so I thought there was a way we could figure out how to make this on our own," Nathaniel says humbly. Using plans he found on the internet, Nathaniel built a winnower that worked just as well and saved him several thousand dollars.

After the winnower, the nibs are ground in a machine between two large granite stones. Organic cane sugar is mixed with the crushed nibs, and the heat from the stones rubbing together causes the nibs to liquefy. Nathaniel compares this stage of the process to making peanut butter, slowly, over time.

The chocolate is then aged in blocks for two to five weeks before being tempered and placed into molds for the bars.

If all of this technical jargon and equipment sounds intimidating, it was for Nathaniel at first too. Claiming to have not been much of a math or science student during his formative years, Nathaniel chose to forego a college education to pursue his dream of owning his own business. After much trial and error, physics, chemistry, and algebra started becoming second nature.

"I always told the kids that came in here, 'When I was your age I thought I would never use chemistry or math, but you never know what you are going to do when you grow up,'" Nathaniel laughs.

Nathaniel also used his marketing and sales skills. The bars came wrapped in gold foil, for a little Willy Wonka nostalgia, and artful, modern papers that resembled gift wrap. This was all by design.

"If you were going to spend your money on one of our chocolate bars, I wanted you to feel like you were getting an experience," says Nathaniel.

Nathaniel was an artist and his Hillcrest shop, a chocolate studio. A minimalist space, reminiscent of an artist's loft, kept the focus on the product and the purity of the process.

"I wanted to be the best and push to the limit to see what I was capable of," says Nathaniel. "We wanted to not only let consumers taste where each bar came from, but we hoped to educate them as well."

Nathaniel was also partnered with other food providers in Central Arkansas to create some unique products. Izard provided chocolate for a chocolate stout at Lost Forty Brewing and collaborated with Loblolly Creamery (see page 30) on an ice cream. They locally sourced pecans from Barnhill Orchards (see page 12) for their popular bourbon pecan caramels and used liquor from Rock Town Distillery for specialty chocolate creations.

"Central Arkansas has been very supportive and is one of the main reasons I did this," says Nathaniel.

Nathaniel admits finding time for himself was a challenge. Being the sole employee and in the store every day, there was little time left over for him to have much of a personal life, and he is still in his twenties.

"I had been here for five years, and I was still in that getting-the-train-moving phase. I had good times, chugging along, and sometimes it was slow. As a small business owner, you have times of high motivation and then there are times where you just say, 'Man, I'm worn out.'"

In June of 2018, Nathaniel traveled to Guatemala where he met the farmers producing cacao for his Guatemalan bar. It was an eye-opening experience. Nathaniel saw the many villagers working the farm and how they all worked together to make a living, one that would be considered quite poor by American standards. This experience reinvigorated Nathaniel in his continued push to buy fair trade and to support the entire chain of his business, from farmer to consumer. Taking a major trip also reminded Nathaniel that he had taken few since starting the business, and though he loved his business, there were other passions being neglected.

Nathaniel made the difficult decision to close the business in 2019, after his most profitable year yet in 2018. It will be exciting to see what the future brings for Nathaniel. Central Arkansas may see this young entrepreneur again in a new role.

———

Location: Little Rock
Known for: Gourmet chocolates, truffles, and caramels

RATCHFORD BUFFALO FARMS

L.C. Ratchford stops his vehicle—an older model SUV that he uses to give tours to friends and family—and points at signs wild hogs have been in the area. The high point in the cattle pasture is rife with scuffed grass and trees marked with mud left behind from hogs rubbing against them. With a quirk of his ever-present grin, he describes his ongoing method of dealing with the invasive animals. It involves making them into sausage.

L.C. grew up on this property with his brothers and sisters, and he's added to it substantially over the years. His mother, known as Granny Madge, worked on the land when it was the largest strawberry farm in Arkansas, though there's not an obvious strawberry patch to be seen there now. Instead, buffalo graze the fields.

When L.C. was a child, he saw buffalo on television and decided then and there that he would raise them one day. But first, he became a welder. The job allowed him to save up money to eventually start Ratchford Buffalo Farms in Marshall. It also gave him a skill set much needed on the farm. If a buffalo bull leans on a barbwire fence to scratch himself, he'd likely tip the whole fence. Instead, L.C. has installed countless feet of welded pipe fencing, which is exactly what it sounds like. Sections of metal pipe, about six inches in diameter, are fused together to make a stronger fence. "It's incalculable how much money I've saved, being able to weld."

If they come upon a vehicle with its windows down, buffalo cows stick their heads right in the open windows. Without calves around, the creatures are as docile as any cow, and they know the vehicle means treats. L.C. and special guests fill their hands with large feed pellets, and the muscular, sandpaper tongues reach out to lick up the snack. The cows are beautiful, but it's the buffalo bulls that impress with their sheer size. They're taller than six feet at the head, and their impressive manes remind one of an old Western.

But of course, they're not a novelty—they're a farm animal.

Ground buffalo meat and jerky sticks from Ratchford Farms can be found all over Arkansas, and the flavor complements any dish in which one would normally use ground beef.

Like many farmers, L.C. is interested in conservation and sustainability. He points to his natural springs and the way they're routed to drinking areas for the bovine and buffalo cattle, but also focuses on using the resources he has in a way that will protect and improve them.

L.C.'s home—complete with a second story he rebuilt himself after a small fire destroyed it— is gated like the rest of the farm. To one side, he has a small permaculture garden with fruit trees and berries as the star of the show. To the back is something different. As he raises an exotic animal, he's found himself in touch with people who, he says, get in over their heads, and so he has developed quite the collection. "I'll get a call that someone bought an animal they weren't ready to care for safely, and I'll wind up going and getting it." To that end, he has peacocks, a pot-bellied pig, a couple of goats, a llama, and—the perpetual favorite—a deer that is no longer able to live in the wild. It eats from visitors' hands and, much like a dog, gives a signal that it would like to play by rearing up on its back legs or tapping with its front hooves. The animals live in a small pasture where they are provided safety, room to romp, and friends to spend their time with.

It's clear that L.C. truly enjoys what he does. He certainly makes his living from farming, so it's a job. But it's also a calling, the thing he loves most. "I wouldn't want to live anywhere else or do anything else."

——

Location: Marshall
Known for: Buffalo meat, jerky snack sticks
Site: ratchfordfarms.net
Social: ⨍@Ratchford-Buffalo-Farms

WYE MOUNTAIN MUSHROOMS

"This strain in particular is so pretty," Jess Wilkins says, kneeling to get closer to the white, shaggy shape of a Lion's Mane mushroom that's nearly ready to be harvested.

Jess's appreciation for mushrooms is clear. While it's reasonable to imagine growing mushrooms as something more akin to collecting mushrooms on a stroll through the woods, or perhaps a special log kept in the backyard on which a reliable strain can be counted upon to grow each year, the reality of growing mushrooms to sell is altogether different. When Jess kneels to inspect his crop, he's kneeling beside a tall shelf installed in a specially outfitted cooler, properly referred to in the business as a fruiting chamber.

Eight or nine years ago, Jess started growing his own pearl oyster and Lion's Mane mushrooms in a small Tupperware container. "I was just curious about it. It was a hobby. My girlfriend at the time was a server, and she mentioned what I was doing to the chef. He said, 'Hey, bring 'em up here. I'll buy 'em.'" It was that first sale that led Jess to believe there might be a hole in the market. As he cooked at different restaurants over the years, his awareness of the gap grew.

He started learning about the different species of mushrooms, growing them, and tinkering with ways to cook them. He quickly realized their value. The taste, he says, is incomparable to store-bought mushrooms—richer, bolder, and the scent, more aromatic. When he let other people try them, they gave similar feedback.

"I believe wholeheartedly in this product. It is so good," he says. But with that passion comes what he refers to as "heartbreak" when things don't go as planned. It takes an average of four to eight weeks, sometimes longer, for mushrooms to be ready to eat once the growth medium is inoculated with spawn, and if the crop doesn't pan out, it can be a tough loss to manage. "If you don't do it right, you lose everything. You're counting on the results and then you don't get them . . . It's a let down on many levels." Worse even than potential financial setbacks is the feeling of personal failure. "I sort of take it personally. It adds insult to injury. It's broken my heart a couple of times."

Lion's Mane, one of Jess' favorite mushrooms, is, in a word, "weird." He says that while it's one of the easiest mushrooms to grow—it has a wider acceptable temperature and CO_2 range that many other varieties—the result growers get can be completely related to the strain of Lion's Mane they have. The new strain Jess is trying would triple the weight he is getting for the same amount of effort.

Though Lion's Mane, a rather large mushroom, is delicious and out-of-this-world gorgeous, it's smaller chestnut mushrooms that Jess thinks are choice. Even if they are allowed to grow a bit longer than might be ideal, they don't get tough or chewy. "The cap stays delicious the whole time, but the stem gets a little bit more texture to it. It never gets rubbery, and it's definitely still good." That said, he usually tries to cut them a bit on the younger side, which makes for a better presentation when cooked whole.

Three years ago, Jess started trying to grow mushrooms commercially, though he shakes his head at the amount of time lost to mistakes. "It's not like I should have known any better. I just learned the hard way." It's because of his experiences that he plans, aside from growing and selling mushrooms, to offer consulting to other aspiring mushroom growers. He'd still sell spawn, but also visit potential growers' sites, write out the designs they'll need for their goals, and give feedback on problems encountered. He points out that paying him for his time and knowledge could save others time, heartache, and money. "I made enough mistakes to screw it up, though I saved my ass. I've been fortunate enough to bail myself out, and if you're tighter on funds than I am, you wouldn't have made it."

To grow mushrooms at a commercial scale requires the right setup. The lab space at the front of Jess's fruiting chamber is insulated to provide a temperature-stable workspace for sterilizing and plugging mushrooms into substrate. The fruiting chamber, lined with rows of metal shelves, is where the plugged blocks of substrate live while the mushrooms are growing. When it's time to harvest, he comes along with a paper sack and cuts off the mature mushrooms. Some strains allow for additional flushes of growth before the substrate will be sterilized and replugged.

When the substrate—blocks of even, graded wood—runs out of nutrients and can no longer produce a viable crop, it's replaced, but not discarded. Those used blocks make great additions to a backyard compost pile, where the living material left in the block starts consuming itself and the pile gets hot. "It's like black gold," Jess says fondly.

Though Jess would eventually like to produce 800 pounds of mushrooms each week, he says that because of the cost to expand to that level of production, he's taking his time to develop plans he's certain will result in success. "There's a difference between sterilizing fifty blocks at once or 500 at once. My current setup is pretty good and pretty efficient for its size. The design I'm planning should maintain that efficiency."

Jess has been working as a handyman for about three years—something that's clear in the new cedar stair and porch rail on the front of his home. It's not store-bought wood. He cut the saplings, let them cure, then cut and installed them himself.

In the summer of 2018, he turned a corner. While he still helps two or three clients, the mushroom business provides his primary income. And by the summer of 2019, he hopes to be well on his way to scaling that 800-pound-per-week goal.

———

Location: Little Rock
Known for: Lion's Mane mushrooms
Social: ❶@Wyemountainmushroomfarm
⬤@Wye_mountain_mushroom_farm

ROZARK HILLS COFFEE ROASTERIE

Rita Fox grew up in Seattle, where her father owned an industrial fabrication business. When customers had a need for a piece of equipment that didn't yet exist, they would come to her father, who would design and build it for them.

One day, three young men brought an old, worn-out coffee roaster to Rita's father, asking if he could fix it. He did, and they went on to found a coffee chain—Starbucks.

After Starbucks started the gourmet coffee craze, many people, especially in the Pacific Northwest, wanted to jump on the coffee bandwagon. Rita's father was inundated with work—people needed a roaster built, rebuilt, or installed—and Rita's family has been in the coffee business ever since.

After her dad retired, he sold the business to Rita's husband, Marty, and began to travel. Her parents wandered the country for a few years, coming through Arkansas several times. The last time they came through the state, her dad said to her mother, "If God were to come to earth, this is where God would come." So, when they were ready to settle once more, they found eighty acres in Rose Bud and proceeded to build a house. "It took them three years to single-handedly build that house," Rita says. They built the cabinets, the trusses, ran their own electrical, constructed a barn, and put up fences.

Rita and her husband still lived in Seattle. When they came down for a visit, her dad told them, "There's no reason why you have to live in Seattle. You kids could move to Arkansas." To sweeten the deal, her father continued, Rita and her parents could start a coffee roastery.

It took six months to make the decision, but after giving their employees in Seattle a generous two-year notice, the couple began preparing for the move. Two years later, they sold off their fabrication equipment and moved to Arkansas.

The first step in roasting a new coffee is to test roast it. Rita collects samples of new coffees and does a sample roast, which brings out the best characteristics of the bean—chocolatey, fruity, or nutty. But, a sample roast also brings out the faults of the beans. After allowing the beans a day to degas, Rita takes them into the cupping room and taste-tests

the coffee. "We cup them blind, score them, and the ones that score best, we order."

A variety of factors impact the bean—was it grown in shade? Was it fertilized? How and when was it trimmed? To make sure Rita gets the bean she wants, she orders based on lot numbers. Sacks range from 132 to 154 pounds, depending on the country of origin. In 2017, RoZark roasted 65,000 pounds of beans.

"You're always playing with the rules," Rita says. "You're always tasting your coffee, trying to keep it consistent. Just because he (Chad, RoZark's roaster) has a Costa Rican he's perfected, doesn't mean the next lot of Costa Rican will be roasted in the same way. Each crop changes a little bit," she explains.

As a gourmet coffee roaster, RoZark can only source beans that score an eighty or higher (on a scale of 1-100) on the score sheet curated by the Specialty Coffee Association of America.

Chad, the RoZark roaster, has been with the company since 2009, and Rita roasted for the twelve preceding years. Roasting, in fact, is Rita's favorite part of the coffee business. When Chad goes on vacation, Rita is happy to fill in, though, she says, it does cause her to get behind on the other parts of her business.

"Roasting," Rita says, "is definitely an artisanal skill. For example, Ethiopian has some really great blueberry notes. By roasting it, Chad can diminish those blueberry notes and hide them or pull out something completely different." Some beans are harder, while some are softer. Some respond better to a lighter roast—being roasted for less time, possibly at a lower temperature—while some beans' flavors are better developed with a dark roast. Chad listens to the coffee roasting, to the cracking sound the beans make as they roast. The scent changes; the color changes.

When he determines the beans are finished, which takes around fourteen minutes depending on your method, beans are dumped into the cooling tray, which has a blower attached. This allows beans to cool from roughly 380 degrees to less than one hundred degrees in about two minutes.

It took Rita years to learn this delicate process herself. Rita was a waitress for much of her life, but she also worked in a group home for developmentally disabled adults for several years before going to work at a missile factory. Finally, she began helping her husband install coffee roasters. One day, his secretary announced her plans to marry. Marty lost his secretary. Rita offered to help until he found another secretary, but he never quite managed to do so.

Being a waitress, secretary, and a coffee roaster are all a far cry from her childhood dream—veterinary medicine. That plan only lasted until her horse became ill. To get well, he needed one shot weekly for about a month. "Mom said, 'Why don't you just give Jack the shot, and we don't have to pay the veterinarian to come out and give him his shot every week?'" The first time Rita tried to stick the needle in his flank, she followed the vet's instructions exactly: she patted his flank several times with her knuckles before finally turning her hand to insert the needle. The horse flinched just a bit, as one might

expect—but his movement startled Rita, and she jerked the needle back out. The vet had to make a return trip, and Rita's future in animal medicine was deemed unlikely.

The initial challenge in moving to the South from the coffee capital of the United States was that, here, not everyone drank gourmet coffee. Particularly twenty years ago, Rita says, it was as though people were scared of gourmet coffee. When they first began roasting, people would often walk through the door and ask, "We're just curious . . . What are you doing here?" After explaining, Rita would often offer a small sample for them to take home. "I'd say, 'Here, let me give you some coffee to take home.' They would respond, 'Oh, no, I don't drink that kind of coffee. I only drink Folgers.'"

One man all but refused to take her sample, which ruffled Rita's feathers. "I said, 'You know what? If you don't like it, throw it away. Better yet, give it to somebody who might like it. If you don't like it, don't drink it!'" It took several weeks, but he eventually reappeared, having tried the sample she gave him, and asked if he could purchase more.

Though RoZark began with wholesale-exclusive sales, that didn't stop passers-by from dropping in to ask if they could purchase a couple pounds of coffee to take home. After a few years of turning people away, Rita's dad suggested turning the front half of the office into a retail space. After all, turning away customers isn't good business practice.

Though Rita has been a coffee roaster for over two decades, she says the more time goes by, the more she enjoys it. Her palate is ever-improving. She still attends the Specialty Coffee Association of America (SCAA) convention every year, and every year she goes to every cupping event she can. "I'm always trying to find something that makes me go, 'Oh!' I'm always looking for that holy grail. I always want to try and find a better coffee, something more unique," she says.

Rita's preferred coffee blend changes depending on her mood. Sometimes, she wants something that explodes in her mouth, in which case she gravitates to a Kenyan bean. But, "There's times when I just want to be chill and mellow, so I go with a Brazilian."

———

Location: Rose Bud
Known for: Organic and conventionally-grown coffee
Site: rozark.com
Social: ⓕ@rozarkhills

DUNBAR GARDEN

Students at Gibbs Elementary and Dunbar Middle School in Little Rock have something very unique: their own secret garden, hidden from the road on the edge of downtown. Accessed through a gated arbor sandwiched on two acres between the schools sits the Dunbar Garden, a playground for the senses where kids can stain their lips purple with mulberries plucked from trees, hear the rumble of a 1950s tractor, pet bunnies, and learn the stages, and smells, of compost. Dunbar Garden is not only open to students, it is a nonprofit teaching garden, open to the public. The garden, which began in 1992, encourages "planting ideas to grow minds," and the goal of Dunbar Garden is to educate people on where food comes from and how to grow it oneself.

The garden averages about 800 school kids per month when the weather is nice. When the garden began, it was in-school suspension students who were sent out to do the work to help build the garden. It has since taken off, unique in that this is an inner-city school with ample space for a garden to grow.

Damian Thompson, who ran the garden from 2004–2018, knows all about the impact this garden has on visitors and the lessons it can teach. A former student at Dunbar Middle, Damian believes the garden teaches children a valuable work ethic as well as how to care for their environment.

"The kids love coming out here. They help pull all the weeds, ready the soil, move the compost, and plant the seeds. That's one of the pushes out here—you don't get to stop for the summer. You have to keep working on a farm."

The garden also lets students just be kids, offering an outdoor venue for them to get their energy out, get their hands dirty, and learn at the same time. The animals and plants often offer good old-fashioned potty humor. The garden used to have goats, but they are now cared for by Heifer Urban Farm (see page 36). Students loved when the male goats would urinate on each other's faces and beards, a common practice. They also get a good laugh from a hardy plant named mullein that grows throughout the garden. Also known as cowboy toilet paper, this plant has a tall stalk with bushy leaves, making it a perfect last resort resource in the woods.

This relaxed attitude of trying new things and experimentation is what students love about Dunbar. Students turn the compost with a pitchfork and watch the temperature, which can easily reach 100 degrees, with a thermometer.

Damian will put water bottles in the compost to heat them up before the students come out, and when they arrive the water looks like hot coffee steaming from the heat of the compost. "They learn about renewable resources, renewable energy, how it heats up, and what you could do with that heat," says Damian.

Students can also try their hand at beekeeping. The hive is a popular attraction at Dunbar Garden. One student is usually selected to become the beekeeper and gets to put on a bee suit and open up the hive. Students love to come watch the bees swarm, and the honey produced is used as fundraiser for the garden.

"People wait for it and they will ask when the honey is coming," Damian admits. "We get seven or eight gallons per year and will sell it for $1 per ounce. It is typically sold through word of mouth."

Dunbar Garden sells mainly at the garden market stand to neighbors. Along with the honey, they sell beeswax, homemade hot sauces, salves, and of course, produce. Funds from market sales pay for garden upkeep.

Dunbar Garden also holds fundraisers, weddings, and events throughout the year. Events are becoming a big business, and one can see why. The garden has many eye-catching attractions. One is the hops tunnel. Hops grow vertically, and at Dunbar Garden the hops grow along a lengthy trellis that makes a beautiful, scented tunnel. The tunnel is marked with a mosaic made by the art class and is popular for students to run through and for dinners to be hosted under. One of Damian's fondest memories is when two of his students, whose parents started Flyway Brewing, gave him a lesson in hops.

"Two kids at Gibbs parents are owners at Flyway. They came out and told us *all* about hops," Damian laughs. "The arbor looks big, but the amount of hops it grows is not much."

The hops are sold mostly to local homebrewers, who will trade on beer futures, donating beer for fundraising events at Dunbar Garden.

Every inch of the garden is used. Food trees including peaches, muscadines, pecans, figs, and chestnuts pepper the garden. A chicken coop hosts the garden's chickens where students collect eggs, and a large greenhouse stores early stage plants.

Looking to the future of the garden, the goal is to move to a permaculture model, which is more sustainable. Audrey Long, the new executive director, has big plans to implement more perennial plants and introduce simple 30-inch beds. "Every plant needs to serve two or three purposes," says Audrey. "Weeds become snacks for the chickens. We have golden rod, a perennial, growing along the fence line that's medicinal, beautiful, and used in our flower arrangements. For me, the key is to continue growing more perennial plants and have more designated easier-care areas so you don't have to do all of this." (She sweeps her hand to indicate volunteers working hard at weeding).

Having worked as one of these weeding volunteers for years through Arkansas GardenCorps, a division of AmeriCorps, Audrey is familiar with the garden and the volunteers and visitors that regularly stop by. She is constantly moving between her duties managing the garden to visiting with and selling produce to walk-in neighbors. The kids are always fresh on her mind when organizing the garden, though.

"We have twelve-year-olds, with their size-twelve shoes, and they will walk on anything and not even notice. So we put the newspaper down and covered it with wood chips so they have a walkway," laughs Audrey.

She hopes to teach students and adults that you really don't need much to grow your own food, and the benefits can lead to a healthier life. Audrey would know. Before starting at Dunbar Garden, she moved back to her hometown of Pine Bluff to care for her mother who had been recently diagnosed with dementia. Having read that certain minerals and fats could combat dementia, she started making kale smoothies and upping coconut oil in her mother's diet (see recipe page 77). After costly trips back and forth to Little Rock, Audrey decided to grow her own food in her mother's front yard, starting with mustard greens and homemade container gardens on the patio.

"I still have those jokers today," exclaims Audrey. "It started with that and questioning what can I do to be healthier and it not be extremely expensive. Mother earth provides plenty."

At its heart, education is what Dunbar Garden is all about. Encouraging kids to spend more time outdoors and away from screens, even if the occasional middle schooler forgets it's garden day and has to cover his fancy tennis shoes with a plastic Kroger shopping bag, Dunbar Garden is a place where students learn through fun. The most rewarding part of the garden for Damian is when a student comes back to visit.

"It will make you feel real old, but it's cool to have the students come back in. Someone will walk in here, and I'll go 'It's been eight years? WHAT? You've got a beard!'"

———

Location: Little Rock
Known as: A teaching garden
Site: dunbargarden.org
Social: 🐦@DunbarGarden 📷@dunbar_garden

BEN POPE

When deciding where to relocate from Texas, Arkansas was definitely on Ben Pope's radar. He was no stranger to the Central Arkansas gardening community, having lived here briefly before moving on.

"The gardening community is what brought me back. There is such a strong community here and everyone is connected. I don't know anywhere else this exists."

Ben Joined the Arkansas GardenCorps, a statewide AmeriCorps program, in 2016 and accepted the position as the Arkansas Children's Hospital garden servicemember. "An underdeveloped program with potential," Ben was looking to push himself and make some big life changes. He had just left his job as a technical writer, along with the comfort of a desk and a strong paycheck, for a new city and new industry, one subject to weather disruptions, bug infestations, and physical labor.

Ben was confident he could handle it. Working tirelessly, he broke new ground and doubled the garden's output from 1,437 pounds of produce to 2,852 pounds in one year. This number is important. After all, the garden began following an ACH and UAMS survey which found that twenty percent of families entering the ACH emergency room had difficulty accessing food. Doubling the output meant a major impact on the families and neighbors that used the garden for fresh produce.

"I felt I was ready for that," says Ben. "I was ready to grow a really big garden."

Arkansas is one of the leading states in food insecurity. Children are especially impacted, and childhood obesity is a leading health concern in the state. One of the most popular days at the garden, Thursday, is free farm stand day where anyone can come by and get a free bag of produce.

Most of the food from the garden goes to the Helping Hand pantry. The garden is supported by many neighbors and volunteers. A true community effort, the garden is all about repurposing items when possible and using what's available, like transforming an industrial sink from one of AHC's surgical suites into a place for washing produce and hands. Ben and

his business partner, Jimmy Parks, repurpose billboard tarps as weed barriers. They turn them over, advertising side facing down. The vinyl works great for gardening projects.

In August 2018, when Arkansas GardenCorps was temporarily suspended, many service members were left with immense knowledge and skills but nowhere to put them to use. Fortunately, several of the GardenCorps clients took over the gardens on their own, coming up with their own funding and resources. Ben partnered with service member Jimmy Parks, who has been instrumental in the Promise Garden on 12th Street. They created Foment, LLC, a word which literally means to stir things up or incite. Foment was created to serve as a for-hire labor force to assist with community gardens and as a resource for backyard gardeners helping procure seeds and compost and assisting with building projects like raised beds and chicken coops. Foment now has the Centennial Garden at ACH, the Mabelvale Middle School garden, the Promise Garden, and the Youth Home Garden as clients.

Ben believes GardenCorps will likely return in some form, and believes its impact is still being felt in Central Arkansas.

"It has had a positive legacy. There are a dozen former members still here with gardening, teaching, and community engagement experience. All that is essential to developing and maintaining community gardens. It's been a real positive, even if it doesn't come back."

Ben, who has a master's degree in history, and Jimmy, who has a PhD in public health, joke that they are "two way over-educated gardeners," but they are able to teach lessons to visiting students on how to grow food and also talk about the relationship between soil health, plant health, and human health. The knowledge they bring to the community is working to foment a movement in the Central Arkansas gardening space.

——

Location: Little Rock
Known for: Growing for those in need in the surrounding community
Site: archildrens.org/health-and-wellness/community-outreach/community-garden

ACCESS GARDEN

ACCESS®, a non-profit serving Arkansas families, offers evaluation, education, therapy, and vocational training for children and young adults with special needs. One of the activities considered a core mission of ACCESS is therapy and vocational training through the horticulture program. Executive Director Tammy Simmons, who co-founded ACCESS twenty-five years ago, grew up surrounded by her family's greenhouses in Pine Bluff and understood the important sense of independence fostered by growing your own food. She was determined to incorporate gardening and being outdoors into the ACCESS curriculum. Today, students as young as kindergarten age work the garden alongside Tammy's mother, Norma, and her brother Scott.

Krysten Levin, Marketing and Special Events Manager, says she sees younger kids trying new things through the garden and believes it is particularly impactful on students with food issues, a common challenge for ACCESS students.

"It started with a small opportunity to supplement curriculum and therapy and has blossomed into this huge program that allows ACCESS to work with the community."

The annual ACCESS plant sale is a community mainstay. Local gardeners, neighbors, and even commercial landscapers attend the sale supporting the services provided by ACCESS. It is also an opportunity to interact with the students, and a valuable social and vocational experience for the students who run the sale.

When ACCESS expanded to a second campus a few years ago, the horticulture program gained additional land, allowing them to try their hand at hydroponics, growing herbs and microgreens using organic-based principles. With a new greenhouse, the H.O.P.E. (Herbs Offering Personal Enrichment) program in partnership with Taziki's Mediterranean Café was developed. Seven paid interns, all students in ACCESS young adult programs, grow, weigh, package, and deliver herbs and greens to three Taziki's locations.

"Taziki's takes a lot of pride in knowing the [intern] growers," says Krysten. "The interns take a lot of pride in basically running a small business."

Other restaurants, including Table 28, Petit & Keet, and Diane's Gourmet are purchasing herbs and greens from the students. Being able to earn a wage gives these young adults independence and life skills that are enormously transferable in the job market.

_____

Location: Little Rock
Known for: Education, therapy, training, and activities for children and youths with learning disabilities
Site: accessgroupinc.org
Social: 🅕🅞 @accessgroupinc

FARM GIRL MEATS

Katie Short is a devotee of food systems biology—that much is clear. The conversation around food, community, and human relationships to both started when she was a child in California. She says, "I've always been really interested in science and biology and systems. I started cutting class in high school to go to the little regional display farm, and I was also interested in the bigger mechanisms behind it all."

Despite the famous growing climate in California, Katie chose to come to Arkansas to study farming. Katie laughs kindly when she says, "It was almost like going back in time, coming here. I'd be having conversations with people and they'd ask, 'Now, what is pesto?'" She continues, "There's a real sharp learning curve in farming, and the food system is already so fully developed in California." This leaves little space for new farmers to come in and make real change.

Katie came, like many burgeoning farmers, to Heifer Ranch in Perryville (see page 36), where she spent two years, eventually running their livestock department. They not only put up interns in housing, they also provided a stipend, making it an attractive opportunity for young farmers looking to learn. Today, Katie says, the opportunities are ever-increasing, and access to similar resources is becoming easier to find. "If you want to intern somewhere, there are whole Listservs, and none of that existed fifteen years ago," Katie explains.

After a couple years at Heifer, Katie used lessons learned at Heifer Ranch to act on her childhood dreams. In 2005, she was able to lease seventeen acres from Heifer on which to properly begin Farm Girl Meats with a couple of friends. It was around this time that she began dating Travis Short, her now former husband.

Travis was born in Ohio, where his interest in raising animals started as a young boy. Travis got his first flock of sheep when he was twelve years old, and he often helped his relatives on their operations. "I was the extra set of hands to help bale hay or clean out barns or pour concrete or whatever needed to be done." When he made the decision to come work at Heifer Ranch in 1995, he was living in

Wyoming, working seven miles outside of Yellowstone on a dude ranch. Travis volunteered at Heifer Ranch for about four years, and during that time, he ran a small cow-calf operation with a friend and eventually sold meat through the River Market farmers' market.

By 2008, the friends with whom Katie began Farm Girl Meats had moved on to other projects, and Katie and Travis had added two daughters to their family. By 2015, their production needs had outgrown their total property of forty-seven acres—conveniently, as it turns out, because their lease at Heifer Ranch ended at about the same time. Around then, Travis, who still worked a day job in construction, heard through the grapevine about a local guy who'd been talking about selling his 130 acres. They quickly struck a deal.

Once they'd moved to the new property, Travis began construction on the farmhouse, and Farm Girl Meats held a Kickstarter campaign to plant around 2,000 trees in the front of the valley. Those trees all produce fruit or nuts, including hazelnuts, chestnuts, persimmons, apples, and pears. Eventually, there will be a whole forest where livestock, particularly pigs, can mostly feed themselves.

This single farm project has resulted in hundreds of hours spent learning how the parts of a forest work together. For example, hardwoods like to grow up in tight environments. Brush brings humidity to the forest and stabilizes the temperature. The goal for planting so many trees is part of a larger plan to reduce outside inputs, such as bought feed, but also allow the animals to express themselves in a more natural way, resulting in a more satisfied life. Of course, the benefit for humans is that this method also produces rich, tender, flavorful meat.

"We have to make a lot of compromises for agriculture. It baffles me how we've gotten to a place where the animals have given up everything and the people have also given up the good stuff! Is it really worth it to have no flavor? That is one of the best parts of this, to me—the difference in the quality of your life if the things you put in your mouth are deeply satisfying," Katie said.

Katie and Travis have since ended their relationship, but Travis maintains a vision for the farm that's in line with its fourteen-year history. "I would say the vision for the farm is the same, just accelerated. We had a rough five or six year plan for me to get out of construction, but being on the farm now I can do a lot of things I didn't have time to do before," Travis says.

Currently, Farm Girl services restaurants along with their farm share program. The number of restaurants varies from two regulars up to six or eight, depending on the season and availability, with kBird—serving Thai street food in Little Rock—being their most consistent customer. About twenty percent of Farm Girl's business is wholesale; thirty percent comes from the meat share, and the rest comes from the farmer's market. There are two share seasons that total a whole year. In an effort to provide food for people with as many dietary needs as possible, their sausage is gluten-free, and they have some nightshade-free options.

> "That is one of the best parts of this, to me—the difference in the quality of your life if the things you put in your mouth are deeply satisfying."

Farm Girl Meats raises Corriente or Corriente-cross cattle, one of the oldest breeds in the Americas. They came over in 1493 after being dumped on the coast of Florida by Spanish ships, and are, at this point, nativized. Katie says, "We chose them because they fit our ideas about production. We want animals that are smaller to medium frame; those tend to be more efficient with grass, especially, but also in hot, humid climates, animals with large horns do better because their horns are vascularized. It's like an elephant's ear, giving more surface area to cool. It's a built-in cooling system."

The cattle are moved every day to fresh pasture. The winding treeline may appear random, but Farm Girl Meat's sustainability efforts are anything but. The pasture was precisely plotted with a laser level and subsoiled to help with water catchment.

Because the farm doesn't bring in stock from outside sources, Farm Girl's cattle is limited to what comes out of their breeding stock. A decision to raise more beef means waiting four years for heifers to mature. Pigs, on the other hand, can be bred at ten months old, and so they can be scaled more quickly.

For the first several years they farmed pigs and let the breeding herd do almost whatever they wanted, but results were mixed. Sometimes, the sows would decide to birth in a ditch. After observing several litters and taking notes about the kind of nests the sows preferred, Katie designed custom sow houses. "They're on skids, so we can pull them around to wherever the pigs are. They have a rail on the inside so mom has something to lean against and won't squish the babies. There's a gap at the back in case we need to hang a heat lamp or something."

The pigs are divided into groups. Some are breeding stock without piglets, some are mothers with piglets, and still others are being grown out for butcher. The breeding area gets heavy use from the presence of a large pig family, and so Farm Girl rests each area used for breeding for at least a year so the area can fully recover between uses. It's due to that care that Travis says simply, "I'm very confident in our pork."

The group is led by Roslyn, a 700-pound sow who is both incredibly lovely and incredibly large. Because it's important that pigs, who are very social creatures, lead a stable social life, Roslyn lives permanently with several other females, though she is the matriarch.

The grown pigs are their own kind of beautiful, but it's the piglets that cause visitors to crouch in the grass. The arrival of visitors has the piglets' mothers calling them to hide in the grass on the edge of their pen. Quiet voices and lowered bodies encourage the piglets to come close. Katie says it best, "They're red pigs in bright green grass—it doesn't get any better than that."

Toward the house is a group of between 500 and 750 Freedom Ranger chickens. They're in movable pens, so they have constant access to fresh pasture. Freedom Rangers take eleven weeks to reach the same size industrially-raised chickens reach in six weeks. "You couldn't raise Cornish Cross chickens, like I do, with the doors open. They would just stay inside. Or, they might get out a bit, but they wouldn't go back inside when it's raining, and they wouldn't know to avoid hawks or other predators." Instead, Travis says, it's the sunshine, fresh air, and access to the outdoors that makes chickens and other animals healthy—that makes them real animals.

Travis says doing anything outside is the best part of farming, whether it's moving animals or anything else. The weather, of course, can sometimes be brutal, but a little advance planning usually allows for inside work on those days.

Raising meat isn't as simple as feeding the animals and taking them to the butcher at the appropriate time. With three animal enterprises, pick-up and drop-off at the butcher, wholesale accounts, farmer's markets, and a meat share to manage, it can be difficult to manage everything. "The farming part is the easiest thing. Almost anybody can feed a pig or raise a chicken. It's getting that product in a presentable state to a customer who wants to buy it." And that's not counting the marketing that's required to maintain a successful business.

That's why, Travis says, marketing and developing new markets is his most difficult daily task, but acknowledges that will be different six months or a year from now, because if there's one constant, it's change. "And, I mean, there's a balance too. You don't want to market more than you can produce. But you don't want to produce more than you can market. So either the freezers are too full and you're trying to find room for something, or they're empty and you're trying to find something to put in the meat share."

Both sets of Travis's grandparents and all of his uncles ranched. "Cattle to sheep to goats to, you know, any kind of animal. It was before Tyson or any of those companies, so everyone owned everything in their operation. My grandpa raised turkeys for years in the woods, which I always quiz my mom about. I'm like, 'How did he do this? How did he do that?'"

————

Location: Perryville
Known for: Bratwursts
Site: farmgirlfood.com
Social: ⓕ@Farm-Girl-Meats ⓘ@pvillefarmgirl

A FEW RECIPES

Mother's Royal Alkaline Smoothie
Made for Audrey Long's mother, Dr. Earlene C. Larry (1939–2014)

3 cups frozen prickly pear cactus fruit (an antioxidant-rich plant Audrey used regularly in Arizona but that can be grown in Arkansas) or fresh fruit
3–5 ice cubes
1–2 cups apple juice, coconut milk, or water
1 scoop vanilla protein mix (hemp or whey protein)
1 teaspoon Himalayan or Black Sea salt (to taste)
2 tablespoons local honey or stevia (to taste)
1/2 teaspoon cinnamon (to taste)
1 teaspoon turmeric
Garnish with fresh mint

Roast ripe prickly pear fruit when it's freshly picked to easily remove the needles. Freeze for later use. Mix all ingredients in blender and blend.

Protein mix will make this a meal teeming with rich antioxidants.

Daley Family Chocolate Chip Cookies

2 cups flour
1 ½ teaspoon baking soda
1 ½ teaspoon salt
¾ cup butter (softened)
1 cup brown sugar
½ cup granulated sugar
1 egg
1 egg yolk
1 tablespoon vanilla
2 cups chocolate chips

Sift together flour, baking soda, and salt, then set aside. Cream together softened butter, brown sugar, and granulated sugar. Once creamed, add egg, egg yolk, and vanilla. Next, slowly stir in dry ingredients until well mixed.

Once mixed, add chocolate chips. When batter is made, scoop cookies onto a sheet and place in the refrigerator until chilled. Bake at 350 degrees for 12–15 minutes. Best served warm with a glass of cold milk.

Ratchford Chili

2 pounds ground buffalo meat
1 ounce chili powder
12 ounces stewed tomatoes
½ quart fresh tomato juice (L.C. uses his mother's top-secret recipe)
12 ounces cooked red beans
Worcestershire sauce (to taste)
Salt (to taste)

Combine all ingredients in a slow cooker and cook on high for 4–6 hours. Serve warm and top with shredded cheese, sour cream, and corn chips or cornbread.

Barnhill Orchards Strawberry Jam

5 cups crushed/blended Barnhill Orchards' strawberries (about 8 cups whole berries)
7 cups sugar
1 teaspoon butter (optional; this reduces foam produced during the cooking process)
1 box Sure Jell

Sterilize jam jars and lids by simmering in boiling water for at least 10 minutes while the jam is cooking.

Add crushed strawberries, Sure Jell, and butter into a large saucepan over medium heat.
Bring mixture to rolling boil. Add sugar and stir constantly. Return to full, rolling boil for one minute, then remove from heat.

Skim the foam layer off the top with a metal spoon (the foam is delicious and can be eaten, but doesn't look good in the canning jars, so put in separate bowl).

Ladle the mixture into sterilized jars, leaving ¼ inch of space at the top of the jar. Wipe the rims and threads with a clean cloth, then cover with two-piece lids. Place jars in canner. Water must cover the tops by 2 inches. Cover the canner and bring the water to a boil.

Process the jam jars for 10 minutes and remove. Place upright on a towel or cooling rack, allowing them to sit for 24 hours. After the jars cool, check to ensure for proper sealing by pressing the center of the lids. If the lid springs back, it is not sealed and requires refrigeration.

ACKNOWLEDGMENTS

FROM THE AUTHORS

One of our very favorite things to do is go on a good old-fashioned farm tour. This project wouldn't have been possible without all the wonderful people who welcomed us to their farms, kitchens, and shops and gave us their version of that farm tour. We appreciate all of you so much.

And of course, a big thank you to our photographer, Philip Thomas of Novo Studio. Philip, you can always be counted on to traipse through mud, rain, and cow poop in pursuit of the best photo possible.

We also owe a big thanks to publisher Erin Wood, designer Amy Ashford, and proofreader Kaitlin Lowe. It takes a village.

FROM SARA

When I met Lacey almost ten years ago, I knew immediately she was a friend. During this process, we have spent every week together, sharing thoughts, writing, and going through life. It has been essential.

Thank you to the 10 x 12 book club for being a strong, supportive group of women, and to my steadfast friends who have humored this project, and others, for years.

Finally, to my parents and family, thank you for your ears, your love, and your example. Jack and Brinkley, you make me happy. Jay, thank you for picking up extra dad duty, becoming a second editor, serving as my one-man focus group, and being my constant cheerleader.

FROM LACEY

My biggest thank you goes to Sara, without whom I'd still be sitting around thinking, "Hmm, wouldn't this be a fun book to write . . ." You feed me when I'm hangry, push me to get things done, snap me back to earth when I get distracted by shiny new ideas, and somehow manage to wrangle those ideas into something that works.

To my family and friends-who-are-family: you make this life sweet. Thanks for existing.

They say writing the book is the easy part, and they're right. I couldn't have imagined how much help it takes to get a book project ready to print, and I'm so grateful to all the help we had along the way.

OTHER TITLES FROM ET ALIA PRESS

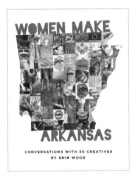

Meet fifty women—including a fire performer, a hatter, a kombucha brewer, and an aspiring time traveler—who will challenge the way you think about what it takes to lead a creative life as they reveal how they hush negative voices, channel intuition, and bear out their visions. Let the failures, victories, and wisdom of these bold creatives help you step into creative freedom. *Featured in the 2019 Arkansas Literary Festival.*
8.5 x 11, standard color paperback with 250+ images. 200 pages. $29.95.

Explore concepts of art, history, and the feminine as you conjure the lives and habits of 20th century American women through the purses they carried. *What's Inside: A Century of Women and Handbags, 1900–1999* by Anita Davis compliments the permanent exhibition of ESSE Museum & Store, one of only three purse museums in the world. *Featured in the 2019 Arkansas Literary Festival.*
8.5 x 9 premium color paperback. 55+ images and illustrations. 118 pages. $29.95.

Be riveted by 150+ micro images and stories of *100 Insects of Arkansas and the Midsouth* like The Fiery Searcher, The Twice-Stabbed Lady Beetle, and the Ambush Bug. As you peek under leaf litter, learn to identify what flies across your path, listen for sounds on summer nights, and study insect weaponry and mimicry with Norman and Cheryl Lavers, prepare for your woodland walks to be forever changed. 8.5 x 9 premium color paperback. 106 pages. $26.95.

With the hope of encouraging adoption of rescue dogs and raising awareness of issues surrounding their care, *Home Sweet Home: Arkansas Rescue Dogs & Their Stories* by Grace Vest, with photographs by Whitney Bowers, shares the images and stories of twenty-five Arkansas rescue dogs. Inspired by her own furry family members, Vest shows how the choice to adopt can rescue canines and humans alike. *Featured in the 2018 Arkansas Literary Festival.* 8.5 x 9 Premium color paperback. 82 pages. $24.95.

CPSIA information can be obtained
at www.ICGtesting.com
Printed in the USA
BVHW022302070619
550490BV00001B/1/P